THE MISSION OF THIS GENERATION

THE MISSION OF THIS GENERATION

A Compilation & Study Guide
of Messages from
the Universal House of Justice
to Bahá'í Youth

Compiled by the
European Bahá'í Youth Council

Bahá'í
Publishing Trust
27 Rutland Gate, London SW7 1PD

The Mission of This Generation:
A Compilation & Study Guide
of Messages from
the Universal House of Justice
to Bahá'í Youth

Compiled by the European Bahá'í Youth Council

© 1996 The Bahá'í Publishing Trust
27 Rutland Gate
London SW7 1PD

British Library Cataloguing-in-Publication Data

A catalogue record for this book
is available from the British Library

ISBN 1-870989-72-4

Designed and typeset at the Bahá'í Publishing Trust, UK

O Thou kind Lord! We are servants of Thy Threshold, taking shelter at Thy holy Door. We seek no refuge save only this strong pillar, turn nowhere for a haven but unto Thy safe-keeping. Protect us, bless us, support us, make us such that we shall love but Thy good pleasure, utter only praise, follow only the pathway of truth, that we may become rich enough to dispense with all save Thee, and receive our gifts from the sea of Thy beneficence, that we may ever strive to exalt Thy Cause and to spread Thy sweet savours far and wide, that we may become oblivious of self and occupied only with Thee, and disown all else and be caught up in Thee.

O Thou Provider, O Thou Forgiver! Grant us Thy grace and loving-kindness, Thy gifts and Thy bestowals, and sustain us, that we may attain our goal. Thou art the Powerful, the Able, the Knower, the Seer; and verily, Thou art the Generous, and, verily, Thou art the All-Merciful, and verily, Thou art the Ever-Forgiving, He to whom repentance is due, He Who forgiveth even the most grievous of sins.

`Abdu'l-Bahá

Acknowledgements

The European Bahá'í Youth Council is grateful to Mr Kasra Mottahedeh for collecting the messages; to Mr Shahriar Razavi for the formulation of the questions; and to the Bahá'í Publishing Trust of the United Kingdom for its editorial advice.

Preface

It is easy to see that society is declining. As young Bahá'ís, we are confronted by ways of life and sets of values very different from the Bahá'í model. These same patterns of individual life are present everywhere as social, economic and political crises. The Universal House of Justice says that this generation enjoys 'a unique distinction' because we live 'in a period when the forces of history are moving to a climax, when mankind will see the establishment of the Lesser Peace'.[1] This special time in history is linked with extraordinary changes in the spiritual condition of the world. As Bahá'í youth, we can affect the course of events by using the creative power and energy 'stimulated by awareness of

---

1. From the Universal House of Justice to the participants of the European Youth Conference in Innsbruck, 4 July 1983.

the approaching end of the twentieth century'.[2] We can channel these spiritual forces to make a difference to the world in our own lifetime, and thereby 'contribute significantly to shaping the societies of the coming century'.[2]

Knowing how to respond to such a challenge is often confusing. How do we begin to play our part? What does it mean for our personal lives, our social lives, our education and careers?

Bahá'í youth are especially blessed to have received many messages from the Universal House of Justice telling us just how to respond to the special needs of our time. This guidance is a precious gift which reminds young people of the fundamental priorities of our lives at this critical time in the social development of our planet.

The purpose of this compilation is to facilitate a more systematic study of this wealth of guidance. To this end, for the first time all the messages of the Universal House of Justice addressed to the Bahá'í youth of the world, together with the most significant of other letters and messages addressed to specific groups of youth gathered in conference at times of particular moment, or to institutions dealing with youth matters are gathered in one volume. Access to these messages should assist

---

1. From the Universal House of Justice to the Bahá'í youth of the world, 3 January 1984.

2. Ibid.

Bahá'í youth everywhere in making decisions and plans for the future, and enable each one to develop his or her own understanding of the mission of this generation.

So we offer this compilation and study guide, in the hope that it will assist you in fulfilling your role as a young Bahá'í at this unique time in history, and inspire you to continued service to the Blessed Beauty throughout your lives.

***

This book is a project of the European Bahá'í Youth Council, an institution appointed by the Universal House of Justice. The Council is charged with providing a continental perspective on the activities of Bahá'í youth in Europe, addressing their needs and assisting them in understanding their role, and in facing the many challenges of living as a young person at this time.

Contents

Section 2: Major Themes

Introduction

The young followers of Bahá'u'lláh are especially favoured to have been the recipients of the continuous guidance of the Institution ordained by Him to steer His community. Ever since its earliest years, the Universal House of Justice has directed special attention to Bahá'í youth, addressing them collectively on the many issues confronting them in the discharge of their distinctive and sacred mission. As we read these unique messages, we find dazzling historical analysis, clear exposition of the decisive role of youth at this critical moment of transition in the evolution of the planet, clarion calls to spiritual battle, but, above all, encouragement, assurance and love from the divine institution which is the tender parent of every young Bahá'í.

The compilation consists of two sections: first, the full text of the messages, without annotation or comment, each followed by nine simple study questions. Section two is a thematic arrangement of extracts from the messages. The purpose of this second section is to facilitate reference to important recurring themes in the guidance of the Universal House of

Justice. So as to enrich the understanding of a particular theme, references to other passages in the Bahá'í Writings, as well as other messages of the Universal House of Justice have also been provided.

It is hoped that this compilation will play a part in advancing the vision for a new movement among this generation of Bahá'í youth, by clearly presenting our sacred mission, and inspiring our hearts to a deeper dedication. With a clear sense of purpose, with determination and creativity, we can become part of a 'mighty mobilisation of youth' and play a decisive role in the spiritual future of our society.

Using this book as a study guide

There are three kinds of questions on each text. These are intended not only to interrogate the messages themselves, but also to invite reflection on the application and implications of the guidance of the Universal House of Justice for one's own life.

The first of these levels ('meaning') explores the basic understanding of the meaning of words and sentences: answers can be found in the text itself. The next level ('application') invites the reader to identify the application of the concepts to his or her own circumstances. The final level ('implication') probes the concepts for other situations and circumstances. The number of the paragraph which has prompted the question is usually given in parentheses. However, this does not mean that the answer to the question is necessarily in the text, as many questions are intended to promote further reflection on the personal implications of these messages.

These questions are by no means exhaustive. Rather, they point to one method of systematic study which progressively explores and practically applies the guidance contained in these messages. It may also be an effective tool to aid group study.

Devising your own questions

The student may devise additional questions at one or more of the three levels, to suit his or her individual needs. If used for group study, each member may be asked to think of a new question at each level, or to give examples of application and implication. Both individual students and groups may also like to consider ways in which these messages relate to the plan in which the Bahá'í community is currently engaged, and which their local and National Spiritual Assemblies have outlined. It may also be helpful for the student to consult with the local Spiritual Assembly, Auxiliary Board member or assistant about how the guidance contained in these messages can be put into practice.

Further study

Recent Ridván messages from the Universal House of Justice to the Bahá'ís of the world offer a greater understanding of the society in which this generation of Bahá'í youth live. These messages identify the positive and negative forces at work in our world, address the greatest challenges of our time, and anticipate the arrival of the Lesser Peace. Those who wish to deepen their understanding of the mission of Bahá'í youth in relation to the work of the Bahá'í community in the wider world will benefit from studying these messages alongside the guidance contained in this compilation.

Section One:

Messages to Bahá'í Youth

[1]

10 June 1966

To Bahá'í Youth in Every Land

1   In country after country the achievements of Bahá'í youth are increasingly advancing the work of the Nine Year Plan and arousing the admiration of their fellow believers. From the very beginning of the Bahá'í Era, youth have played a vital part in the promulgation of God's Revelation. The Báb Himself was but twenty-five years old when He declared His Mission, while many of the Letters of the Living were even younger. The Master, as a very young man, was called upon to shoulder heavy responsibilities in the service of His Father in 'Iraq and Turkey; and His brother, the Purest Branch, yielded up his life to God in the Most Great Prison at the age of twenty-two that the servants of God might 'be quickened, and all that dwell on earth be united.' Shoghi Effendi was a student at Oxford when called to the throne of his Guardianship, and many of the Knights of Bahá'u'lláh, who won imperishable fame during the Ten Year Crusade, were young people. Let it, therefore, never be imagined that youth must await their years of maturity before they can render invaluable services to the Cause of God.

2 For any person, whether Bahá'í or not, his youthful years are those in which he will make many decisions which will set the course of his life. In these years he is most likely to choose his life's work, complete his education, begin to earn his own living, marry, and start to raise his own family. Most important of all, it is during this period that the mind is most questing and that the spiritual values that will guide the person's future behaviour are adopted. These factors present Bahá'í youth with their greatest opportunities, their greatest challenges, and their greatest tests — opportunities to truly apprehend the teachings of their Faith and to give them to their contemporaries, challenges to overcome the pressures of the world and to provide leadership for their and succeeding generations, and tests enabling them to exemplify in their lives the high moral standards set forth in the Bahá'í writings. Indeed, the Guardian wrote of the Bahá'í youth that it is they 'who can contribute so decisively to the virility, the purity, and the driving force of the life of the Bahá'í community and upon whom must depend the future orientation of its destiny, and the complete unfoldment of the potentialities with which God has endowed it.'

3 Those who now are in their teens and twenties are faced with a special challenge and can seize an opportunity that is unique in human history. During the Ten Year Crusade — the ninth part of that majestic process described so vividly by our beloved Guardian — the community of the Most Great Name spread with the speed of lightning over the major territories and islands of the globe, increased manifoldly its manpower and resources, saw the beginning of the entry of the peoples by troops

into the Cause of God, and completed the structure of the Administrative Order of Bahá'u'lláh. Now, firmly established in the world, the Cause, in the opening years of the tenth part of that same process, is perceptibly emerging from the obscurity that has, for the most part, shrouded it since its inception and is arising to challenge the outworn concepts of a corrupt society and proclaim the solution for the agonizing problems of a disordered humanity. During the lifetime of those who are now young the condition of the world, and the place of the Bahá'í Cause in it, will change immeasurably, for we are entering a highly critical phase in this era of transition.

4   Three great fields of service lie open before young Bahá'ís, in which they will simultaneously be remaking the character of human society and preparing themselves for the work they can undertake later in their lives.

5   First, the foundation of all their other accomplishments, is their study of the teachings, the spiritualization of their lives, and the forming of their characters in accordance with the standards of Bahá'u'lláh. As the moral standards of the people around us collapse and decay, whether of the centuries-old civilizations of the East, the more recent cultures of Christendom and Islam, or of the rapidly changing tribal societies of the world, the Bahá'ís must increasingly stand out as pillars of righteousness and forbearance. The life of a Bahá'í will be characterized by truthfulness and decency; he will walk uprightly among his fellowmen, dependent upon none save God, yet linked by bonds of love and brotherhood with all mankind; he will be entirely detached from the loose standards, the decadent theories, the

frenetic experimentation, the desperation of present-day society, will look upon his neighbours with a bright and friendly face, and be a beacon light and a haven for all those who would emulate his strength of character and assurance of soul.

6   The second field of service, which is linked intimately with the first, is teaching the Faith, particularly to their fellow youth, among whom are some of the most open and seeking minds in the world. Not yet having acquired all the responsibilities of a family or a long-established home and job, youth can the more easily choose where they will live and study or work. In the world at large young people travel hither and thither seeking amusement, education, and experiences. Bahá'í youth, bearing the incomparable treasure of the Word of God for this Day, can harness this mobility into service for mankind and can choose their places of residence, their areas of travel, and their types of work with the goal in mind of how they can best serve the Faith.

7   The third field of service is the preparation by youth for their later years. It is the obligation of a Bahá'í to educate his children; likewise it is the duty of the children to acquire knowledge of the arts and sciences and to learn a trade or a profession whereby they, in turn, can earn their living and support their families. This, for a Bahá'í youth, is in itself a service to God, a service, moreover, which can be combined with teaching the Faith and often with pioneering. The Bahá'í community will need men and women of many skills and qualifications; for, as it grows in size the sphere of its activities in the life of society will increase and diversify. Let Bahá'í youth,

therefore, consider the best ways in which they can use and develop their native abilities for the service of mankind and the Cause of God, whether this be as farmers, teachers, doctors, artisans, musicians, or any one of the multitude of livelihoods that are open to them.

8   When studying at school or university Bahá'í youth will often find themselves in the unusual and slightly embarrassing position of having a more profound insight into a subject than their instructors. The Teachings of Bahá'u'lláh throw light on so many aspects of human life and knowledge that a Bahá'í must learn, earlier than most, to weigh the information that is given to him rather than to accept it blindly. A Bahá'í has the advantage of the Divine Revelation for this age, which shines like a searchlight on so many problems that baffle modern thinkers; he must therefore develop the ability to learn everything from those around him, showing proper humility before his teachers, but always relating what he hears to the Bahá'í teachings, for they will enable him to sort out the gold from the dross of human error.

9   Paralleling the growth of his inner life through prayer, meditation, service, and study of the teachings, Bahá'í youth have the opportunity to learn in practice the very functioning of the Order of Bahá'u'lláh. Through taking part in conferences and summer schools as well as Nineteen Day Feasts, and in service on committees, they can develop the wonderful skill of Bahá'í consultation, thus tracing new paths of human corporate action. Consultation is no easy skill to learn, requiring as it does the subjugation of all egotism and unruly passions, the cultivation of

frankness and freedom of thought as well as courtesy, openness of mind, and wholehearted acquiescence in a majority decision. In this field Bahá'í youth may demonstrate the efficiency, the vigour, the access of unity which arise from true consultation and, by contrast, demonstrate the futility of partisanship, lobbying, debate, secret diplomacy, and unilateral action which characterize modern affairs. Youth also take part in the life of the Bahá'í community as a whole and promote a society in which all generations — elderly, middle-aged, youth, children — are fully integrated and make up an organic whole. By refusing to carry over the antagonisms and mistrust between the generations which perplex and bedevil modern society, they will again demonstrate the healing and life-giving nature of their religion.

10   The Nine Year Plan has just entered its third year. The youth have already played a vital part in winning its goals. We now call upon them, with great love and highest hopes and the assurance of our fervent prayers, to consider, individually and in consultation, wherever they live and whatever their circumstances, those steps which they should take now to deepen themselves in their knowledge of the Divine Message, to develop their characters after the pattern of the Master, to acquire those skills, trades, and professions in which they can best serve God and man, to intensify their service to the Cause of Bahá'u'lláh, and to radiate its Message to the seekers among their contemporaries.

The Universal House of Justice

Questions [1]

Meaning

1. Which examples of service to the Cause of God rendered at a young age are cited here? (paragraph 1)
2. What is the process of which the Ten Year Crusade constituted the ninth part? (paragraph 3)
3. What are the three fields of service referred to in this message? (paragraphs 5-7)

Application

1. How do the factors presenting opportunities, challenges and tests affect your life? How could you respond to them? (paragraph 2)
2. In what particular fields of study have you found that the Faith gives you greater insight than your teacher? How could you meet the challenge which this presents? (paragraph 8)
3. How can Bahá'í youth plan to render service in each of the three areas highlighted in this message? (paragraphs 5 to 7)

Implication

1. How can the Bahá'í community become a 'beacon light'? (paragraphs 5, 9)
2. How can we improve the way we learn the functioning of the World Order of Bahá'u'lláh? (paragraph 9)
3. What are the applications of true consultation? (paragraph 9)

[2]

9 October 1968

To the Bahá'í Youth in Every Land

1   In the two years since we last addressed the youth of the Bahá'í world many remarkable advances have been made in the fortunes of the Faith. Not the least of these is the enrolment under the banner of Bahá'u'lláh of a growing army of young men and women eager to serve His Cause. The zeal, the enthusiasm, the steadfastness and the devotion of the youth in every land has brought great joy and assurance to our hearts.

2   During the last days of August and the first days of September, when nearly two thousand believers from all over the world gathered in the Holy Land to commemorate the Centenary of Bahá'u'lláh's arrival on these sacred shores, we had an opportunity to observe at first hand those qualities of good character, selfless service and determined effort exemplified in the youth who served as volunteer helpers, and we wish to express our gratitude for their loving assistance and for their example.

3   Many of them offered to pioneer, but one perplexing question recurred: Shall I continue my education, or should I pioneer now? Undoubtedly this same question is in the mind of every young Bahá'í wishing to dedicate his life to the advancement of the Faith. There is no stock answer which applies to all situations; the beloved Guardian gave different answers to different individuals on this question. Obviously circumstances vary with each individual case. Each individual must decide how he can best serve the Cause. In making this decision, it will be helpful to weigh the following factors:

4   Upon becoming a Bahá'í one's whole life is, or should become devoted to the progress of the Cause of God, and every talent or faculty he possesses is ultimately committed to this overriding life objective. Within this framework he must consider, among other things, whether by continuing his education now he can be a more effective pioneer later, or alternatively whether the urgent need for pioneers, while possibilities for teaching are still open, outweighs an anticipated increase in effectiveness. This is not an easy decision, since oftentimes the spirit which prompts the pioneering offer is more important than one's academic attainments. One's liability for military service may be a factor in timing the offer of pioneer service.

5   One may have outstanding obligations to others, including those who may be dependent on him for support. It may be possible to combine a pioneer project with a continuing educational program. Consideration may also be given to the possibility that a pioneering experience, even though it interrupts

the formal educational program, may prove beneficial in the long run in that studies would later be resumed with a more mature outlook. The urgency of a particular goal which one is especially qualified to fill and for which there are no other offers. The fact that the need for pioneers will undoubtedly be with us for many generations to come, and that therefore there will be many calls in future for pioneering service.

6   The principle of consultation also applies. One may have the obligation to consult others, such as one's parents, one's Local and National Assemblies, and the pioneering committees.

7   Finally, bearing in mind the principle of sacrificial service and the unfailing promises Bahá'u'lláh ordained for those who arise to serve His Cause, one should pray and meditate on what his course of action will be. Indeed, it often happens that the answer will be found in no other way.

8   We assure the youth that we are mindful of the many important decisions they must make as they tread the path of service to Bahá'u'lláh. We will offer our ardent supplications at the Holy Threshold that all will be divinely guided and that they will attract the blessings of the All-Merciful.

The Universal House of Justice

Questions [2]

Meaning

1. What qualities of youth are highlighted here? (paragraph 1)
2. What factors should be considered when deciding how best to serve the Cause? (paragraphs 4-11)
3. What are the most urgent pioneer goals for your country? (paragraph 8)

Application

1. What actions do you intend to take to increase your own effectiveness for future service? (paragraph 4)
2. How could you explore the possibility of combining 'a pioneer project with a continuing education programme'? (paragraph 7)
3. In what fields of service can you visualize yourself?

Implication

1. What special services could a young pioneer render? (paragraph 3)
2. How can the principle of consultation be employed to arrive at a decision regarding one's future? (paragraph 10)
3. How can prayer and meditation provide guidance? (paragraph 11)

[3]

29 March 1971

*To the European Youth Gathered in Conference in
Namur (Belgium)*

1   The rapidly growing range and effectiveness of the
services of the Bahá'í youth in Europe over the course of the past
few years have given us great encouragement and have raised
high our hopes for the progress of the Cause of God on that
continent.

2   You who are now gathered in Namur in response to the
call sent out by the Continental Board of Counsellors have been
made responsible for working out the next stages of this
audacious campaign, within the framework already agreed
between Counsellors and the National Spiritual Assemblies, and
you may be sure that our prayers will surround you as we
supplicate the Blessed Beauty to inspire your deliberations, unite
your hearts and fire your enthusiasm so that there may go out
from this conference a ringing call, carefully conceived plans and
clearly stated objectives, that will not only galvanize the youth of
the continent but, through them, impart a mighty surge forward
to the teaching work of the entire European Bahá'í Community.

3   It is our earnest hope that the outriders of this youthful army of Bahá'u'lláh will win such victories by the time of the Conference in Fiesch as will so inspire the far larger band of young Bahá'ís who will be gathered there that a wave of achievement, which will have already started to roll, will at that conference gain speed and magnitude and revolutionize the progress of the Cause in Europe.

4   Let those who set their hand to this vital enterprise press confidently forward, undeterred by any obstacles which may stand in their way, joyously assured of the unfailing assistance of the conquering power of Bahá'u'lláh, Whom we will supplicate to guide and reinforce every step you take for the promotion of His Cause.

The Universal House of Justice

Questions [3]

Meaning

1. What does 'galvanize' mean? (paragraph 2)

2. What was the hope of the Universal House of Justice for the outcome of this conference? (paragraph 2)

3. What is meant by 'outriders'? (paragraph 3)

Application

1. What plans do you have for serving the Cause? (paragraph 2)

2. What obstacles stand in your way? How will you remove them? (paragraph 4)

3. How could the youth 'impart a mighty surge forward to the teaching work'? (paragraph 2)

Implication

1. Why is it important to have clearly stated objectives in life? (paragraph 2)

2. How could you inspire the 'far larger band of young Bahá'ís'? (paragraph 3)

3. What would constitute a 'revolution' in the progress of the Cause in Europe? (paragraph 3)

[4]

16 July 1971

*To the Bahá'í Youth Assembled at Fiesch
(Switzerland)*

1   The course of history has brought to your generation an unprecedented opportunity and challenge. The rejection of the old world by the youth, in all countries, is shared by Bahá'ís and non-Bahá'ís alike. Unlike your non-Bahá'í contemporaries, however, you have something to put in its place — the World Order of Bahá'u'lláh.

2   That Bahá'í youth are fully capable of meeting the challenge which evolution has placed before them has already been demonstrated. Now, in this conference at Fiesch, as you gird yourselves to launch a campaign in Europe — a continent which has 'entered upon what may well be regarded as the opening phase of a great spiritual revival that bids fair to eclipse any period in its spiritual history' — we urge you to consider that the more you understand the purpose of Bahá'u'lláh and the method by which He will achieve this purpose the greater will be your success.

3   Our hopes for your two-year campaign are boundless, and visualize nothing less than a tremendous forward surge in the

spiritual revival referred to by our beloved Guardian. Our confidence in your ability to perform the task is unshakeable, and we assure you of our firm conviction that your efforts will be assisted by God to the degree to which your supplications and sacrifices are poured forth in His path.

4   Dear friends, we delight in your enthusiasm, admire your accomplishments, give thanks for your dedication and pray that an ever-increasing outpouring of divine bounties and confirmations may reward your efforts in the service of the Blessed Beauty.

The Universal House of Justice

Questions [4]

Meaning

1. What are the conditions of an 'eclipse'? (paragraph 2)
2. What is a 'spiritual revival'? (paragraph 2)
3. What is the 'World Order of Bahá'u'lláh'? (paragraph 1)

Application

1. What unprecedented opportunity faces your generation of youth? (paragraph 1)
2. Why do you think non-Bahá'í youth reject the old world? (paragraph 1)
3. How could we meet the challenge which evolution has placed before us? (paragraphs 2 and 3)

Implication

1. In what aspects of Bahá'í service could we achieve God's assistance? How does this assistance manifest itself? (paragraph 3)
2. What do you think are the things which could be sacrificed? (paragraph 3)
3. How do you understand sacrifice to draw forth divine assistance? (paragraph 3)

[5]

17 March 1983

To Bahá'í Youth Conferences in Costa Rica and Honduras, 31 March - 3 April 1983

1   KINDLY CONVEY FOLLOWING TO BAHA'I YOUTH CONFERENCES IN COSTA RICA AND HONDURAS, 31 MARCH - 3 APRIL 1983. QUOTE WARMLY WELCOME OCCASION SIMULTANEOUS CONFERENCES COSTA RICA AND HONDURAS TO GREET VIBRANT BAHA'I YOUTH CENTRAL AMERICA. YOUR ENTHUSIASTIC EXERTIONS IN SERVICE CAUSE BAHA'U'LLAH AS SHOWN BY SUBSTANTIAL INCREASE YOUR NUMBERS BRING GLADNESS TO OUR HEARTS AND INSPIRE EXHILARATING THOUGHT THAT BRIGHT PROSPECTS SUCCESS LIE IMMEDIATELY BEFORE YOU.

2   YOU MEET AT HIGHLY CRITICAL MOMENT HISTORY WHEN TURMOIL ASSOCIATED WITH THIS ERA OF TRANSITION INTENSIFIES. WITHIN CAUSE ITSELF CAN BE SEEN ON ONE HAND UNPRECEDENTED CAMPAIGN PERSECUTION LONG-SUFFERING IRANIAN BRETHREN AND ON OTHER HAND RESOUNDING TRIUMPHS SEVEN YEAR PLAN INDUCED BY THEIR SACRIFICES AND SYMBOLIZED BY OCCUPANCY PERMANENT SEAT UNIVERSAL HOUSE OF JUSTICE. MANKIND RAPIDLY APPROACHES RECKONING WITH BAHA'U'LLAH'S

INJUNCTION THAT IT BE UNITED. FROM FAR AND NEAR ANGUISHED MULTITUDES CRY FOR PEACE BUT BEING LARGELY IGNORANT HIS LIFE-REDEEMING MESSAGE THEY FEEL NO HOPE. SITUATION THUS PRESENTS BAHA'I YOUTH WITH GREAT OPPORTUNITIES INESCAPABLE CHALLENGE TO RESCUE THEIR PEERS FROM SLOUGH DESPONDENCY POINTING THEM TOWARDS HOPE-RESTORING BANNER MOST GREAT NAME. HOW FITTING THEN THAT YOU SHOULD CONSIDER AT THESE CONFERENCES BEST MEANS EQUIP YOURSELVES SPIRITUALLY TO FULFIL TEACHING MISSION PARTICULARLY SUITED TO YOUR CAPACITIES FOR SERVICE, YOUR ABOUNDING ZEAL AND ENERGY.

3   ARDENTLY SUPPLICATING AT HOLY THRESHOLD ON YOUR BEHALF THAT IN ADDITION TO PRAYING, ABSORBING HOLY PRINCIPLES AND TEACHING THE FAITH, YOU WILL BE SO IMBUED BY BELOVED MASTER'S EXAMPLE SERVICE TO HUMANITY AS TO BE ABLE THROUGH YOUR INDIVIDUAL AND COLLECTIVE DEEDS TO DEMONSTRATE CIVILIZING POWER OUR SACRED CAUSE AND CONVEY VISION ITS SPIRITUAL AND SOCIALLY CONSTRUCTIVE BENEFITS TO YOUR COMPATRIOTS OF ALL AGES.

THE UNIVERSAL HOUSE OF JUSTICE

Questions [5]

Meaning

1. What does 'transition' mean? (paragraph 2)
2. What conditions are associated with an era of transition? (paragraph 2)
3. What do you understand by 'life-redeeming'? (paragraph 2)

Application

1. How could you exhibit the qualities of youth mentioned in this message? (paragraph 2)
2. Why have young people lost hope? (paragraph 2)
3. Give some examples of 'individual and collective deeds' that demonstrate the 'civilizing power' of the Cause. (paragraph 3)

Implication

1. How is mankind's 'reckoning with Bahá'u'lláh's injunction that it be united' reflected in today's society? (paragraph 2)
2. What vision do you convey of the Cause to your peers? (paragraph 3)
3. How do you think carrying out such 'individual and collective deeds' would influence the way your peers view the Faith? (paragraph 3)

[6]

24 June 1983

To Bahá'í Youth Throughout the World

RECENT MARTYRDOMS COURAGEOUS STEADFAST YOUTH IN SHIRAZ, SCENE INAUGURATION MISSION MARTYR-PROPHET, REMINISCENT ACTS VALOUR YOUTHFUL IMMORTALS HEROIC AGE. CONFIDENT BAHA'I YOUTH THIS GENERATION WILL NOT ALLOW THIS FRESH BLOOD SHED ON VERY SOIL WHERE FIRST WAVE PERSECUTION FAITH TOOK PLACE REMAIN UNVINDICATED OR THIS SUBLIME SACRIFICE UNAVAILING. AT THIS HOUR OF AFFLICTION AND GRIEF, AND AS WE APPROACH ANNIVERSARY MARTYRDOM BLESSED BAB CALL ON BAHA'I YOUTH TO REDEDICATE THEMSELVES TO URGENT NEEDS CAUSE BAHA'U'LLAH. LET THEM RECALL BLESSINGS HE PROMISED THOSE WHO IN PRIME OF YOUTH WILL ARISE TO ADORN THEIR HEARTS WITH HIS LOVE AND REMAIN STEADFAST AND FIRM. LET THEM CALL TO MIND EXPECTATIONS MASTER FOR EACH TO BE A FEARLESS LION, A MUSK-LADEN BREEZE WAFTING OVER MEADS VIRTUES. LET THEM MEDITATE OVER UNIQUE QUALITIES YOUTH SO GRAPHICALLY MENTIONED IN WRITINGS GUARDIAN WHO PRAISED THEIR ENTERPRISING AND ADVENTUROUS SPIRIT, AND THEIR

VIGOUR, THEIR ALERTNESS, OPTIMISM AND EAGERNESS, AND THEIR DIVINELY APPOINTED, HOLY AND ENTHRALLING TASKS. WE FERVENTLY PRAY AT SACRED THRESHOLD THAT ARMY OF SPIRITUALLY AWAKENED AND DETERMINED YOUTH MAY IMMEDIATELY ARISE RESPONSE NEEDS PRESENT HOUR DEVOTE IN EVER GREATER MEASURE THEIR VALUED ENERGIES TO PROMOTE BOTH ON HOMEFRONTS AND IN FOREIGN FIELDS, CAUSE THEIR ALL-WATCHFUL AND EXPECTANT LORD. MAY THEY MANIFEST SAME SPIRIT SO RECENTLY EVINCED THEIR MARTYR BRETHREN CRADLE FAITH, SCALE SUCH HEIGHTS OF ENDEAVOURS AS TO BECOME PRIDE THEIR PEERS CONSOLATION HEARTS PERSIAN BELIEVERS, AND DEMONSTRATE THAT THE FLAME HIS OMNIPOTENT HAND HAS KINDLED BURNS EVER BRIGHTER AND THAT ITS LIFE-IMPARTING WARMTH AND RADIANCE SHALL SOON ENVELOP PERMEATE WHOLE EARTH.

THE UNIVERSAL HOUSE OF JUSTICE

Questions [6]

Meaning

1. What does 'martyrdom' mean?

2. What do you understand by 'unvindicated'?

3. What do you understand by 'watchful and expectant Lord'?

Application

1. What are the 'urgent needs of the Cause of Bahá'u'lláh'?

2. What qualities are associated with: a) 'a fearless lion'; b) 'a musk-laden breeze'?

3. How can you apply the admonition to manifest the same spirit evinced by the martyrs?

Implication

1. How could the 'unique qualities of youth' mentioned in this message find expression in the Bahá'í community?

2. What could an 'army of spiritually awakened and determined youth' achieve?

3. What could console the hearts of the Persian believers?

[7]

4 July 1983

To the Participants of the European Youth Conference in Innsbruck

1   With high hopes we greet the representatives of the Bahá'í youth of Europe gathered in conference in Innsbruck. This generation of Bahá'í youth enjoys a unique distinction. You will live your lives in a period when the forces of history are moving to a climax, when mankind will see the establishment of the Lesser Peace, and during which the Cause of God will play an increasingly prominent role in the reconstruction of human society. It is you who will be called upon in the years to come to stand at the helm of the Cause in face of conditions and developments which can, as yet, scarcely be imagined.

2   European Bahá'í youth in particular face tremendous and challenging tasks in the immediate future. Can one doubt that the manner in which the governments of the European nations have rallied to the defence of the persecuted Bahá'ís in Iran will draw down blessings from on high upon this continent? And who among the people of Europe are more likely to be kindled by the challenge and hope of the Message of Bahá'u'lláh than the youth? Now is an opportunity to awaken the interest, set afire the hearts

and enlist the active support of young people of every nation, class and creed in that continent. The key to success in this endeavour is, firstly, to deepen your understanding of the Teachings of the Cause so that you will be able to apply them to the problems of individuals and society, and explain them to your peers in ways that they will understand and welcome; secondly, to strive to model your behaviour in every way after the high standards of honesty, trustworthiness, courage, loyalty, forbearance, purity and spirituality set forth in the Teachings; and above all, to live in continual awareness of the presence and all-conquering power of Bahá'u'lláh, which will enable you to overcome every temptation and surmount every obstacle.

3   A vibrant band of Bahá'í youth on the European continent, committed to the promotion of the Cause of Bahá'u'lláh and the upholding of His laws and principles, determined to work in harmony and unity with their fellow believers of all ages and classes, can revolutionize the progress of the Cause. With a rapid increase in the size of the Bahá'í communities in Europe, the believers of that continent, the cradle of western civilisation, will be the better able to serve as a fountainhead of pioneers, travelling teachers and financial assistants to the Bahá'í communities of the Third World.

4   When deciding what course of training to follow, youth can consider acquiring those skills and professions that will be of benefit in education, rural development, agriculture, economics, technology, health, radio and in many other areas of endeavour that are so urgently needed in the developing countries of the world. You can also devote time in the midst of your studies, or

other activities to, travel teaching or service projects in the Third World.

5   A particular challenge to the Bahá'í Youth of Europe is the vast Eastern half of the continent that is as yet scarcely touched by the light of the Faith of Bahá'u'lláh. It is not easy to settle in those lands, but with ingenuity, determination and reliance upon the confirmations of Bahá'u'lláh, it is certainly possible both to settle and to persevere in service, in goals which demand a spirit of self-sacrifice, detachment and purity of heart worthy of those who would emulate the shining example set by the Martyrs in Iran, so many of whom are youth who have given their lives rather than breathe one word that would be a betrayal of the Trust of God placed upon them.

6   With love and utmost longing we call upon you to immerse yourselves in the Divine Teachings, champion the Cause of God and His Law, and arise for the quickening of mankind.

The Universal House of Justice

Questions [7]

Meaning

1. What does 'standing at the helm' mean? (paragraph 1)

2. What would constitute a 'vibrant band'? (paragraph 3)

3. What are the fields of training in skills and professions mentioned in this message? (paragraph 4)

Application

1. What are some of the tremendous and challenging tasks which the European Bahá'í youth face in the immediate future? (paragraph 2)

2. How can a 'vibrant band' of Bahá'í youth revolutionize the progress of the Cause? (paragraph 3)

3. How could the themes addressed in this letter influence your life?

Implication

1. What are the implications of living in 'continual awareness of the presence and all-conquering power of Bahá'u'lláh' for the teaching work? (paragraph 2)

2. How can Bahá'í youth practise spirituality in their everyday environment?

3. Why are travel teaching and service projects in the Third World important for European youth? (paragraph 3)

[8]

13 December 1983

To Selected National Spiritual Assemblies[1]

1   The Universal House of Justice has been consulting upon aspects of youth service in pioneering throughout the Bahá'í world, and has requested that we convey its views on service in other lands undertaken by Bahá'í youth with voluntary non-sectarian organizations.

2   In the past, the policy adopted by some National Assemblies was to discourage young Bahá'ís from enroling to serve in activities sponsored by non-Bahá'í voluntary organizations, as the Assemblies were under the impression that these young people would not be able to engage in direct teaching, nor participate, for the most part, in Bahá'í activities while serving abroad in such programmes. Perhaps in some instances the Bahá'ís involved were not sure how to function as

---

1. To the National Spiritual Assemblies of the Bahá'ís of Alaska, Australia, Austria, Belgium, Canada, Denmark, Finland, France, Germany, Hawaiian Islands, Iceland, Ireland, Italy, Luxembourg, Netherlands, New Zealand, Norway, Portugal, Spain, Sweden, Switzerland, United Kingdom, and the United States.

members of the Bahá'í community in order to give each aspect of their lives its proper due.

3   In the light of experience, however, it is now clear that we should have no misgivings in encouraging young Bahá'ís to enrol in such voluntary service organization programmes as the United Nations Volunteers, United States Peace Corps, Canadian University Services Overseas (CUSO) and similar Canadian agencies, the British Volunteer Programme (BVP) of the United Kingdom, and other voluntary service organizations. Other countries such as Germany, the Netherlands, and the Scandinavian lands are understood to have similar service organizations which are compatible with Bahá'í development goals as now tentatively envisaged.

4   Some of the advantages of such service to the Faith are worth mentioning. Volunteers will receive thorough orientation and sometimes will be taught basic skills which will enable them to help the Bahá'í community in projects undertaken in developing countries. Wherever they serve, these volunteers should be able to participate in Bahá'í activities, and contribute to the consolidation of the Bahá'í community. The freedom to teach is to a large extent dependent upon the local interpretation of the group leader, but even if volunteers do not engage in direct teaching, being known as Bahá'ís and showing the Bahá'í spirit and attitude towards work and service should attract favourable attention and may, in many instances, be instrumental in attracting individuals to the Faith of Bahá'u'lláh. And finally, the period of overseas service often produces a taste for such service,

and volunteers may well offer to directly promote the pioneer work either in the same country or in another developing country.

5   It is well known that a considerable number of Bahá'ís have already gone abroad to serve with these agencies and that others have espoused the Faith while serving in foreign lands with voluntary service organizations. . . .

6   National Spiritual Assemblies which hold orientation courses for pioneers may benefit from including the subject of rural development in their programmes, and, as in the past, from inviting people who have served in voluntary service organizations to participate in the planning of orientation programmes and in having them share their experiences as volunteer workers in developing countries.

7   The House of Justice expresses the hope that the information contained in this letter will dispel the misunderstandings that have in the past surrounded the question of participation of Bahá'í youth in projects sponsored by non-Bahá'í voluntary organizations.

Department of the Secretariat

Questions [8]

Meaning

1. What is the advice about enrolling in 'voluntary service organization programmes'? (paragraph 3)
2. How might the Faith benefit from such service? (paragraph 4)
3. What may be the effect of 'being known as Bahá'ís and showing the Bahá'í spirit'? (paragraph 4)

Application

1. What 'basic skills' useful for development of the Bahá'í community might be taught in voluntary service organization programmes? (paragraph 4)
2. In what ways might a volunteer 'contribute to the consolidation of the Bahá'í community'? (paragraph 4)
3. Should volunteers 'engage in direct teaching' on projects sponsored by non-Bahá'í voluntary organizations? (paragraph 4)

Implication

1. How might voluntary service with a non-Bahá'í organization affect your life as a Bahá'í youth?
2. What might be the merits of such service for a) the volunteer; b) the Bahá'í community?
3. What challenges might volunteers face in their attempts 'to function as members of the Bahá'í community in order to give each aspect of their lives its proper due'? What are the implications for voluntary service with a non-Bahá'í organization? (paragraph 2)

[9]

3 January 1984

To the Bahá'í Youth of the World

1   The designation of 1985 by the United Nations as International Youth Year opens new vistas for the activities in which the young members of our community are engaged. The hope of the United Nations in thus focusing on youth is to encourage their conscious participation in the affairs of the world through their involvement in international development and such other undertakings and relationships as may aid the realization of their aspirations for a world without war.

2   These expectations reinforce the immediate, vast opportunities begging our attention. To visualize, however imperfectly, the challenges that engage us now, we have only to reflect, in the light of our sacred Writings, upon the confluence of favourable circumstances brought about by the accelerated unfolding of the Divine Plan over nearly five decades, by the untold potencies of the spiritual drama being played out in Iran, and by the creative energy stimulated by awareness of the approaching end of the twentieth century. Undoubtedly, it is

within your power to contribute significantly to shaping the societies of the coming century; youth can move the world.

3   How apt, indeed how exciting, that so portentous an occasion should be presented to you, the young, eager followers of the Blessed Beauty, to enlarge the scope of your endeavours in precisely that arena of action in which you strive so conscientiously to distinguish yourselves! For in the theme proposed by the United Nations — 'Participation, Development, Peace' — can be perceived an affirmation that the goals pursued by you, as Bahá'ís are at heart the very objects of the frenetic searchings of your despairing contemporaries.

4   You are already engaged in the thrust of the Seven Year Plan, which provides the framework for any further course of action you may now be moved by this new opportunity to adopt. International Youth Year will fall within the Plan's next phase; thus the activities you will undertake, and for which you will wish to prepare even now, cannot but enhance your contributions to the vitality of that Plan, while at the same time aiding the proceedings for the Youth Year. Let there be no delay, then, in the vigour of your response.

5   A highlight of this period of the Seven Year Plan has been the phenomenal proclamation accorded the Faith in the wake of the unabating persecutions in Iran; a new interest in its Teachings has been aroused on a wide scale. Simultaneously, more and more people from all strata of society frantically seek their true identity, which is to say, although they would not so plainly admit it, the spiritual meaning of their lives; prominent among these seekers are the young. Not only does this knowledge

open fruitful avenues for Bahá'í initiative, it also indicates to young Bahá'ís a particular responsibility so to teach the Cause and live the life as to give vivid expression to those virtues that would fulfil the spiritual yearning of their peers.

6   For the sake of preserving such virtues much innocent blood has been shed in the past, and much, even today, is being sacrificed in Iran by young and old alike. Consider, for example, the instances in S̲h̲íráz last summer of the six young women, their ages ranging from 18 to 25 years, whose lives were snuffed out by the hangman's noose. All faced attempted inducements to recant their Faith; all refused to deny their Beloved. Look also at the accounts of the astounding fortitude shown over and over again by children and youth who were subjected to the interrogations and abuses of teachers and mullahs and were expelled from school for upholding their beliefs. It, moreover, bears noting that under the restrictions so cruelly imposed on their community, the youth rendered signal services, placing their energies at the disposal of Bahá'í institutions throughout the country. No splendour of speech could give more fitting testimony to their spiritual commitment and fidelity than these pure acts of selflessness and devotion. In virtually no other place on earth is so great a price for faith required of Bahá'ís. Nor could there be found more willing, more radiant bearers of the cup of sacrifice than the valiant Bahá'í youth of Iran. Might it, then, not be reasonably expected that you, the youth and young adults living at such an extraordinary time, witnessing such stirring examples of the valour of your Iranian fellows, and exercising

such freedom of movement, would sally forth, 'unrestrained as the wind,' in the field of Bahá'í action?

7   May you all persevere in your individual efforts to teach the Faith, but with added zest, to study the Writings, but with greater earnestness. May you pursue your education and training for future service to mankind, offering as much of your free time as possible to activities on behalf of the Cause. May those of you already bent on your life's work and who may have already founded families, strive toward becoming the living embodiments of Bahá'í ideals, both in the spiritual nurturing of your families and in your active involvement in the efforts on the home front or abroad in the pioneering field. May all respond to the current demands upon the Faith by displaying a fresh measure of dedication to the tasks at hand.

8   Further to these aspirations is the need for a mighty mobilization of teaching activities reflecting regularity in the patterns of service rendered by young Bahá'ís. The native urge of youth to move from place to place, combined with their abounding zeal, indicates that you can become more deliberately and numerously involved in these activities as travelling teachers. One pattern of this mobilization could be short-term projects, carried out at home or in other lands, dedicated to both teaching the Faith and improving the living conditions of people. Another could be that, while still young and unburdened by family responsibilities, you give attention to the idea of volunteering a set period, say one or two years, to some Bahá'í service, on the home front or abroad, in the teaching or development field. It would accrue to the strength and stability of the community if such patterns could be followed by succeeding generations of youth. Regardless of the modes of service, however, youth must

be understood to be fully engaged, at all times, in all climes and under all conditions. In your varied pursuits you may rest assured of the loving support and guidance of the Bahá'í institutions operating at every level.

9 Our ardent prayers, our unshakable confidence in your ability to succeed, our imperishable love surround you in all you endeavour to do in the path of service to the Blessed Perfection.

The Universal House of Justice

Questions [9]

Meaning

1. What is meant by 'the Divine Plan'? (paragraph 2)
2. What do you understand by the 'confluence of favourable circumstances'? (paragraph 2)
3. What is the admonition of the Universal House of Justice to the Bahá'í youth who are at different stages of life? (paragraph 7)

Application

1. How could you fulfil the 'spiritual yearning of your peers'? (paragraph 5)
2. What plans do you have for serving mankind through your education and training? (paragraph 7)
3. How can you participate in the call for a set period of time dedicated to service to the Cause? (paragraph 8)

Implication

1. What are the implications of entering the arena of service 'unrestrained as the wind'? (paragraph 6)
2. In what ways does the Cause need 'regularity in the patterns of service' by the Bahá'í youth? (paragraph 8)
3. What are the implications of the 'unshakable' confidence of the Universal House of Justice in the ability of the youth to succeed? (paragraph 9)

[10]

24 August 1984

To the Bahá'í Youth Conference in London, Ontario

1   WE HAIL WITH JOY AND HOPE THE ENNOBLING PURPOSES OF YOUR CONFERENCE IN LONDON, ONTARIO. YOU ARE GATHERED AT A MOMENT WHICH RESOUNDS WITH THE SIGNIFICANCES AND CHALLENGES POSED BY THE WORLD-SHAKING EVENTS ENVELOPING THE COMMUNITY OF THE GREATEST NAME IN BAHA'U'LLAH'S NATIVE LAND. THE OUTPOURING GRACE PROVIDENTIALLY VOUCHSAFED THE ONWARD MARCH OF OUR HOLY CAUSE AS A CONSEQUENCE OF THESE EVENTS IS CLEARLY EVIDENT.

2   OUR HEARTS LEAP AT THE INNUMERABLE IMMEDIATE OPPORTUNITIES FOR THE FURTHER UNFOLDMENT OF THE ORDER OF BAHA'U'LLAH TO WHICH UNDOUBTEDLY, YOU CAN AND WILL APPLY YOUR ABUNDANT TALENTS, YOUR ZEST FOR ACTION AND, ABOVE ALL, THE ENTHUSIASM OF YOUR DEVOTION. SURELY, YOU WILL SEE THAT THE HEROIC DEEDS OF SACRIFICE ON THE PART OF YOUR IRANIAN BRETHREN ARE MATCHED WITH CORRESPONDING EFFORTS ON YOUR PART IN THE VAST FIELDS OF TEACHING AND SERVICE LYING OPEN BEFORE YOU.

3   THE EXHORTATIONS ESPECIALLY ADDRESSED TO YOUTH BY OUR BELOVED MASTER AND THE GALVANISING INFLUENCE OF THE GUARDIAN'S GUIDANCE WILL ECHO EVEN MORE LOUDLY IN YOUR HEARTS NOW. INDEED WE WILL PRAY ARDENTLY AT THE HOLY SHRINES THAT YOU MAY REALIZE IN YOUR LIVES THE IDEALS THEY SO PERSISTENTLY UPHELD, THAT YOU MAY THUS 'ACQUIRE BOTH INNER AND OUTER PERFECTIONS' AS YOU INCREASE YOUR STUDY OF THE HEAVENLY WRITINGS, STRIVE TOWARDS EXCELLENCE IN THE SCIENCES AND ARTS AND BECOME KNOWN FOR YOUR INDEPENDENCE OF SPIRIT, YOUR KNOWLEDGE AND YOUR SELF-CONTROL. MAY YOU, AS ABDU'L-BAHA WISHED, BE 'FIRST AMONG THE PURE, THE FREE AND THE WISE.'

THE UNIVERSAL HOUSE OF JUSTICE

Questions [10]

Meaning

1. What is understood by 'ennobling'? (paragraph 1)

2. What is 'independence of spirit'? (paragraph 3)

3. What is meant by 'galvanising'? (paragraph 3)

Application

1. How is 'self-control' applied? How could one increase one's own self-control? (paragraph 3)

2. How could the deeds of our Iranian brethren be 'matched with corresponding efforts'? (paragraph 2)

3. How could you 'apply your abundant talents'? (paragraph 2)

Implication

1. How is acquiring 'inner' perfections related to acquiring 'outer perfections'? (paragraph 3)

2. In which fields of human endeavour could you 'strive towards excellence'? How could this striving be applied within the Bahá'í community? (paragraph 3)

3. How do you understand the admonition to be 'first among the pure, the free and the wise'? (paragraph 3)

[11]

8 May 1985

To the Bahá'í Youth of the World

1   We extend our loving greetings and best wishes to all who will meet in youth conferences yet to be held during International Youth Year. So eager and resourceful have been the responses of the Bahá'í youth in many countries to the challenges of this special year that we are moved to expressions of delight and high hope.

2   We applaud those youth who, in respect of this period, have already engaged in some activity within their national and local communities or in collaboration with their peers in other countries, and call upon them to persevere in their unyielding efforts to acquire spiritual qualities and useful qualifications. For it they do so, the influence of their high-minded motivations will exert itself upon world developments conducive to a productive, progressive and peaceful future.

3   May the youth activities begun this year be a fitting prelude to and an ongoing, significant feature throughout the International Year of Peace, 1986.

4   The present requirements of a Faith whose responsibilities rapidly increase in relation to its rise from obscurity
impose an inescapable duty on the youth to ensure that their lives
reflect to a marked degree the transforming power of the new
Revelation they have embraced. Otherwise, by what example are
the claims of Bahá'u'lláh to be judged? How is His healing
message to be acknowledged by a sceptical humanity if it
produces no noticeable effect upon the young, who are seen to be
among the most energetic, the most pliable and promising
elements in any society?

5   The dark horizon faced by a world which has failed to
recognize the Promised One, the Source of its salvation, acutely
affects the outlook of the younger generations; their distressing
lack of hope and their indulgence in desperate but futile and even
dangerous solutions make a direct claim on the remedial attention
of Bahá'í youth, who, through their knowledge of that Source and
the bright vision with which they have thus been endowed,
cannot hesitate to impart to their despairing fellow youth the
restorative joy, the constructive hope, the radiant assurances of
Bahá'u'lláh's stupendous Revelation.

6   The words, the deeds, the attitudes, the lack of prejudice,
the nobility of character, the high sense of service to others — in
a word, those qualities and actions which distinguish a Bahá'í
must unfailingly characterize their inner life and outer behaviour,
and their interactions with friends or foe.

7   Rejecting the low sights of mediocrity, let them scale the
ascending heights of excellence in all they aspire to do. May they
resolve to elevate the very atmosphere in which they move,

whether it be in the school rooms or halls of higher learning, in their work, their recreation, their Bahá'í activity or social service.

8   Indeed, let them welcome with confidence the challenges awaiting them. Imbued with this excellence and a corresponding humility, with tenacity and a loving servitude, today's youth must move towards the front ranks of the professions, trades, arts and crafts which are necessary to the further progress of humankind — this to ensure that the spirit of the Cause will cast its illumination on all these important areas of human endeavour. Moreover, while aiming at mastering the unifying concepts and swiftly advancing technologies of this era of communications, they can, indeed they must also guarantee the transmittal to the future of those skills which will preserve the marvellous, indispensable achievements of the past. The transformation which is to occur in the functioning of society will certainly depend to a great extent on the effectiveness of the preparations the youth make for the world they will inherit.

9   We commend these thoughts to your private contemplation and to the consultations you conduct about your future.

10   And we offer the assurance of our prayerful remembrances of you, our trust and confidence.

The Universal House of Justice

Questions [11]

Meaning

1. What does 'inescapable' mean? (paragraph 4)

2. What are the 'desperate but futile and even dangerous solutions' which younger generations are indulging in? (paragraph 5)

3. Why should the youth move towards the front ranks? What qualities are required by the youth to do so? (paragraph 8)

Application

1. What aspects of the Cause are people sceptical about? In what practical ways could you vindicate the claims of Bahá'u'lláh? (paragraph 4)

2. What preparations could you make for the world you will inherit? (paragraph 8)

3. What is noble character? How can it be cultivated? (paragraph 6)

Implication

1. How does the influence of the motivations of the youth exert itself on world developments? (paragraph 2)

2. In what situation could our lack of prejudice be manifested? (paragraph 6)

3. What are the implications of rejecting mediocrity for the Bahá'í community? (paragraph 7)

[12]

4 August 1987

To the Participants of the Youth Conference in Manchester

1   LOVING GREETINGS TO PARTICIPANTS OF THIS CONFERENCE CONVENED AT TIME WHEN EUROPEAN BAHA'IS HAVE UNPRECEDENTED OPPORTUNITY DEMONSTRATE POWER FAITH ERADICATE BARRIERS INTERNATIONAL COOPERATION AND INFUSE DYNAMIC OPTIMISTIC QUALITIES INTO COMMUNITY WHICH HAS ALREADY MADE SUCH HISTORIC CONTRIBUTION ADVANCEMENT MANKIND.

2   EUROPEAN BAHA'I YOUTH DISTINGUISHED BY ENERGY VITALITY AND ENTHUSIASM CAN MAKE DISTINCTIVE CONTRIBUTION EMERGENCE FAITH AS PRIMARY AGENT PROMOTING WORLD ORDER AND CIVILISATION.

3   URGE CONFERENCE PARTICIPANTS CONSIDER MEANS BY WHICH YOU CAN SHOW TO PEERS EFFECT OF HIGH MORAL STANDARDS IN PROMOTING TRUE LIBERTY ABIDING HAPPINESS, AND CAN RESTORE TO MANKIND APPRECIATION SPIRITUAL BASIS PURPOSE HUMAN LIFE.

4   ESSENTIAL THAT YOUTH PROLONGED SYSTEMATIC STUDY WRITINGS BELOVED GUARDIAN ACQUIRE PROFOUND UNDERSTANDING OPERATION OF FORCES OF DECLINE AND GROWTH CREATING UNIVERSAL FERMENT IN WORLD TODAY AND LEADING MANKIND FORWARD TO GLORIOUS DESTINY.

5   BURGEONING TEACHING OPPORTUNITIES EUROPE NECESSITATE GREATER EFFORT BELIEVERS CORRELATE TEACHINGS WITH CURRENT THOUGHT AND NEEDS ALL PEOPLE, THUS SHOWING BAHA'I REVELATION SOLE REMEDY INNUMERABLE ILLS AFFLICTING PRESENT SOCIETY.

6   EUROPEAN BAHA'I COMMUNITY HAS DISTINGUISHED RECORD FORMATIVE AGE DEMONSTRATING STRENGTH AND ACTIVITY ITS ADMINISTRATIVE INSTITUTIONS WITH FIDELITY AND PERSEVERANCE ITS ADHERENTS. BY FULL PARTICIPATION IN BAHA'I COMMUNITY LIFE YOUTH CAN FURTHER ENHANCE THIS ENVIABLE RECORD. FROM SEEDS SOWN DURING MANY DECADES DEVOTED EFFORTS TEACHING FAITH, YOUTH CAN NOW GATHER BOUNTIFUL HARVEST.

THE UNIVERSAL HOUSE OF JUSTICE

Questions [12]

Meaning

1. What is meant by 'World Order' and 'World Civilization'? (paragraph 2)

2. What do you understand by 'correlate'? (paragraph 5)

3. What is the 'enviable record' of the European Bahá'í community? (paragraph 6)

Application

1. In what aspects of your life do you demonstrate energy, vitality and enthusiasm? (paragraph 2)

2. What are the specific ways by which we can show our peers the effects of high moral and ethical standards? (paragraph 3)

3. Which aspects of the Bahá'í Teachings could you correlate to the 'current thoughts and needs of all people'? (paragraph 5)

Implication

1. How have the forces of decline and growth affected the Bahá'í community world-wide? How have these forces affected your local community? How have these forces affected your life? (paragraph 4)

2. How can the glorious destiny of mankind be best visualized and communicated? (paragraph 4)

3. Why is participation of Bahá'í youth in community life important? What forms could this participation take? (paragraph 6)

[13]

12 July 1988

*To the National Spiritual Assembly of
The Netherlands in connection with the
International Youth School*

1   We offer our best wishes and our loving greetings to the participants of the Youth School being held at the De Poort Conference Centre in the Netherlands, with the theme 'Living in Europe . . . Our Choices to Serve'.

2   The Bahá'ís of Europe are privileged to be the residents of a region described by the beloved Guardian as 'a continent, occupying such a central and strategic position on the entire planet: so rich and eventful in its history, so diversified in its culture'. For decades the Bahá'í communities in this region have laboured with heroism and devotion, undeterred by the relatively meagre response to their constant endeavours to propagate the message of Bahá'u'lláh.

3   The time has now come for the European believers, most especially the Bahá'í youth, to take full advantage of the growing receptivity to the Bahá'í teachings now evident in Europe. The people of this continent are yearning for the tranquillity, harmony and peace which can be established on an enduring foundation

only through the erection of the World Order of Bahá'u'lláh. Through well-conceived, energetically-pursued and sustained teaching campaigns the youth can hasten the advent of that day when their continent will be blessed with entry by troops and the foundation laid for the spiritual revolution in Europe, anticipated by Shoghi Effendi.

4   We look forward with eager anticipation to European Bahá'í youth arising with a renewed surge of energy and dedication to commit themselves fully in pursuit of the goals of the Six Year Plan. Exciting and challenging vistas are open before them, not only on the homefront of western Europe, but also in eastern Europe where the social changes now occurring must lead eventually to freedom to teach the Faith and establish its institutions. There are vital needs in Africa which the youth in Europe can assist in meeting, renewing and strengthening the historical links binding these two great continents.

5   We are impressed with the Youth School programme, covering a wide range of topics pertaining to the Teachings and their relationship to current thought in Europe, and with the teaching projects which are associated with the School. Our prayers will be offered in the Holy Shrines that this Youth School may be blessed and its participants inspired to carry out mighty deeds in the service of the Beloved of all hearts.

The Universal House of Justice

Questions [13]

Meaning

1. How is Europe described by the beloved Guardian?
(paragraph 2)

2. What are the people of Europe yearning for? (paragraph 3)

3. Which particular arenas of service are presented to the youth
buy the Universal House of Justice? (paragraph 4)

Application

1. How does the commendation of the Universal House of
Justice of the Bahá'í communities in Europe apply to your
community? (paragraph 2)

2. How can the youth fulfill the admonition for teaching
campaigns which are a) 'well-conceived'; b) 'energetically
pursued'; c) 'sustained'? (paragraph 3)

3. What are the current thoughts in Europe? How could the
Teachings be related to these thoughts? (paragraph 5)

Implication

1. How does 'growing receptivity to the Bahá'í teachings'
manifest itself? (paragraph 3)

2. How can the youth participate in bringing about entry by
troops in Europe? (paragraph 3)

3. How does entry by troops presage the 'spiritual revolution in
Europe'? (paragraph 3)

[14]

7 December 1992

To the European Bahá'í Youth Council

1   The Universal House of Justice received a copy of your letter of 31 October 1992 addressed to selected Bahá'ís in Europe seeking their input on the development of a vision for the activities of the European Bahá'í Youth in the Three Year Plan. Accompanying this letter was a very interesting analysis of the current situation of the European Bahá'í youth community.

2   The House of Justice notes that you have shared this correspondence with all the European Counsellors. It feels that it would also be of considerable interest to the National Spiritual Assemblies and suggests that you send copies to them, if you have not already done so.

3   There is one comment that the Universal House of Justice has asked us to make in relation to a number of points made in the analysis, since this may assist in overcoming the problem of the bewildering range of alternatives that lie before youth in these days. This is the importance of conveying to the youth the awareness that every aspect of a person's life is an element of his

or her service to Bahá'u'lláh: the love and respect one has for one's parents; the pursuit of one's education; the nurturing of good health; the acquiring of a trade of profession; one's behaviour towards others and the upholding of a high moral standard; one's marriage and the bringing up of one's children; one's activities in teaching the Faith and the building up the strength of the Bahá'í community, whether this be in such simple matters as attending the Nineteen Day Feast or the observance of the Bahá'í Holy Days, or in more demanding tasks required by service in the administration of the Faith; and, not least, to take time each day to read the Writings and say the Obligatory Prayer, which are the source of growing spiritual strength, understanding, and attachment to God. The concept of the Youth Year of Service should be viewed in this context, as a special service that the youth can devote to the Cause, and which should prove to be a highly valuable element in their own spiritual and intellectual development. It is not an alternative to, or in conflict with, the carrying out of the other vital tasks enumerated above, but rather a unique service and privilege which should be combined with them in the way that is best suited to each individual case.

4   The House of Justice hopes that the discussion you have launched will produce highly significant insights into the current situation and provide you with potent ideas for the activities of the youth in the Three Year Plan.

Department of the Secretariat

Questions [14]

Meaning

1. List the aspects of a person's life which are elements of service to Bahá'u'lláh. (paragraph 3)
2. What is the 'source of growing spiritual strength, understanding, and attachment to God'? (paragraph 3)
3. In what ways should the Youth Year of Service contribute to a youth's development? (paragraph 3)

Application

1. What are some of the 'alternatives that lie before youth in these days'?
2. In what ways can Bahá'í youth show love and respect for their parents?
3. How should a youth decide when to offer a Year of Service?

Implication

1. How should a youth Year of Service volunteer conduct himself/herself?
2. What makes a Year of Service a 'privilege'?
3. Why are the tasks listed in the letter 'vital'?

[15]

17 May 1994

To the youth gathered at the five Regional Bahá'í Youth Conferences in Barcelona, Berlin, Bucharest, St Petersburg & Wolverhampton

1   During this past year, with the encouragement of the European Bahá'í Youth Council, a new movement among this generation of Bahá'í youth has been gathering momentum throughout the continent. Like the swelling of a tide, some waves may be but wavelets as yet, but the time for such an upsurge is here. Surely the successive impulses of training seminars, of the Conference of the National Bahá'í Youth Committees held in April, and now of these five continent-wide conferences, will reinforce the eagerness of the youth to rise and seize the challenge to play their part in reshaping the life of the peoples of the European continent.

2   It is but a century and a half since two young men sat in an upper room of the city of Shíráz; one the Manifestation of God revealing the first Words of God for this era, the other His first disciple. Within the space of six years, both had laid down their lives so that this outpouring of Divine Revelation might quicken all humankind. By that time, hundreds and thousands of eager

hearts, men and women, old and young, rich and poor, learned and illiterate, had arisen to welcome the breaking of the Dawn of Divine Guidance and champion the truth before the world.

3   Now we see that the world has become another world. As Bahá'u'lláh has written: 'Mankind's ordered life hath been revolutionized through the agency of this unique, this wondrous System — the like of which mortal eyes have never witnessed.'

4   You have come together from lands which are troubled by many different ills: ecological, economic, political, social, intellectual and, above all, moral and spiritual. You are aware that some of your peers are desperately seeking solutions and, too often alas, are driven to violent means to combat those immediate evils which fill their vision. Others turn aside, despairingly or cynically from any thought that a remedy is possible. You know the solution, you have the vision, you have the guidance and you are the recipients of the spiritual power which can enable you to triumph over all adversities and bring new life to the youth of Europe.

5   To be young is not easy. There are so many calls on one's time and energy because, not only are you summoned to perform the duties of the day, but also to prepare yourselves for the tasks which will be yours during the remainder of your lives. In weighing how to apportion your time and energy to such a multitude of activities you can all upon the power of consultation with your parents, your friends, and the divinely created institutions of the Bahá'í administration.

6   Those of you who are at a point in your studies or careers where you can devote a special period of service to the Cause of

God, may be able to respond to the call of the Youth Council for an army of youth-year-of-service volunteers to go out after these conferences to accelerate the winning of the goals of the Three Year Plan in Europe. Those who cannot serve in this way, have other avenues of service in their own countries and abroad. For all of you there is the opportunity and the need to present the Teachings of the Cause to all whom you meet, through your character, your behaviour, your unity, your deeds and your words, and to win their allegiance to the Faith.

7   May the Hosts of the Supreme Concourse rush to your aid, and may Bahá'u'lláh bless and guide every step you take for the advancement of His Cause.

8   We shall remember you all in our prayers in the Holy Shrines.

The Universal House of Justice

Questions [15]

Meaning

1. What ills trouble the people of Europe? (paragraph 4)

2. What is the response of young people to the 'evils which fill their vision'? (paragraph 4)

3. What is to be the focus of the 'army of youth-year-of-service volunteers'? (paragraph 6)

Application

1. How are Bahá'í youth equipped to deal with the problems afflicting Europe? (paragraph 4)

2. How could the solution offered by Bahá'u'lláh to these problems be applied? (paragraph 4)

3. How can we better present the 'Teachings of the Cause' through a) our character; b) our behaviour; c) our unity; d) our deeds; e) our words? (paragraph 6)

Implication

1. How can we add to the swelling of the tide of 'a new movement among this generation of Bahá'í youth'? What are the implications of the statement of the Universal House of Justice that 'the time for an upsurge is here'? (paragraph 1)

2. How has the 'wondrous System' brought by Bahá'u'lláh revolutionized 'Mankind's ordered life'? (paragraph 3)

3. How can we offer the message of Bahá'u'lláh to those suffering from cynicism and despair? (paragraph 4)

[16]

22 December 1994

To the National Youth Conference, Phoenix, Arizona

1   We are thrilled that you have gathered in Phoenix to reinforce your efforts during a rising tide of youth activities across your country. The news of the numerous Army of Light projects and Bahá'í Youth Workshops fills us with delight and high expectations. May this conference generate a further mobilization of your energies, such as to break the past records of your individual and collective endeavours to spread the Teachings of Bahá'u'lláh and to conform your lives to His divine purpose. So desired an outcome is necessary if the youth are to contribute decisively to the victory of the Three Year Plan not only in your country but throughout the world in the precious, short time remaining to it.[1]

---

1. *Editor's note:* In a communication on behalf of the Universal House of Justice to the European Bahá'í Youth Council dated 22 March 1995, the Department of the Secretariat of the Bahá'í World Centre states that with respect to this exhortation to contribute to victories 'throughout the world' that it is not applicable to European Bahá'í youth, as they 'are already very active outside their own countries and, indeed, outside the European continent'. The letter also includes a reminder that 'there are vast areas of the eastern part of Europe which need the assistance of youth

2   Relevant also to this necessity is the fact that the period of youth is a fleeting moment; in this brief span, much of what is decided and done by each generation profoundly influences the future of society. Hence, there is no time like now, when the idealism, zeal and enthusiasm which are particular characteristics of youth can be employed to far-reaching benefit. Do not tarry, then, in the steps you must take to shape your future; the current state of humanity imposes too many challenges and opportunities for you to hesitate. The urgency to act is further increased by a looming reality: the youth of today will inherit the responsibilities of the rapidly approaching twenty-first century with all the hopeful prospects foreshadowed in our Writings for the near future.

3   The foundation of your preparation to meet the many unforeseeable changes that will come about rests with your determination and ability to internalize and act upon the divine principles expounded in the literature of our Faith — principles which direct one's inner development and private character, and which guide one's active life of teaching and service. These make for a righteous life — the wellspring of progress for the individual and society as a whole, the harbinger of the very triumph of the Cause of God.

4   By righteous life is not meant an excessive puritanism, but rather a sensible habit of living which, as guided by the Teachings and by the example of `Abdu'l-Bahá, offers a sure path

---

travelling teachers and youth-year-of-service volunteers', and that the Bahá'í youth of Europe have 'many different challenges'.

to attaining the noble purpose for which human beings were created by the Almighty. At this time of trouble and confusion, who can offer a greater demonstration than the Bahá'í youth of the power of righteous living to restore hope to the hopeless and confidence to the fearful among their disillusioned peers?

5   'Cleave unto righteousness, O people of Bahá!' is Bahá'u'lláh's resounding exhortation. 'This', He affirms, 'is the commandment which this Wronged One hath given unto you, and the first choice of His unrestrained Will for every one of you.' The Blessed Beauty's promises in this regard are clear and compelling: 'Valiant acts will ensure the triumph of this Cause, and a saintly character will reinforce its power.'

6   Have no fears or doubts. Your opportunities are great, the confirmations of God abundant. Sally forth, therefore, to seize your moment, to make your mark on the destiny of humankind.

7   Our hopes and prayers surround you.

The Universal House of Justice

Questions [16]

Meaning

1. What 'particular characteristics of youth can be employed to far-reaching benefit'? (paragraph 2)
2. What is the foundation of our 'preparation to meet the many unforeseeable changes that will come about'? (paragraph 3)
3. What is meant by 'righteous life'? (paragraph 4)

Application

1. What are the 'responsibilities of the rapidly approaching twenty-first century'? (paragraph 2)
2. List some of the 'principles which direct one's inner development and private character, and which guide one's active life of teaching and service'. (paragraph 3)
3. How can Bahá'í youth 'restore hope to the hopeless and confidence to the fearful'? (paragraph 4)

Implication

1. What can be the influence of this generation on the future of society?
2. What steps must Bahá'í youth take to shape their own future?
3. How are the efforts of Bahá'í youth to attain 'the noble purpose for which human beings were created by the Almighty' connected to the forces of society? (paragraph 4)

Section Two:

Major Themes

[A]

Inner life &
Personal Transformation

First, the foundation of all their other accomplishments, is their study of the teachings, the spiritualization of their lives, and the forming of their characters in accordance with the standards of Bahá'u'lláh. As the moral standards of the people around us collapse and decay, whether of the centuries-old civilizations of the East, the more recent cultures of Christendom and Islam, or of the rapidly changing tribal societies of the world, the Bahá'ís must increasingly stand out as pillars of righteousness and forbearance. The life of a Bahá'í will be characterized by truthfulness and decency; he will walk uprightly among his fellowmen, dependent upon none save God, yet linked by bonds of love and brotherhood with all mankind; he will be entirely detached from the loose standards, the decadent theories, the frenetic experimentation, the desperation of present-day society, will look upon his neighbours with a bright and friendly face, and be a beacon light and a haven for all those who would emulate his strength of character and assurance of soul.

10 June 1966

* * * * *

ARDENTLY SUPPLICATING AT HOLY THRESHOLD ON YOUR BEHALF THAT IN ADDITION TO PRAYING, ABSORBING HOLY PRINCIPLES AND TEACHING THE FAITH, YOU WILL BE SO IMBUED BY BELOVED MASTER'S EXAMPLE SERVICE TO HUMANITY AS TO BE ABLE THROUGH YOUR INDIVIDUAL AND COLLECTIVE DEEDS TO DEMONSTRATE CIVILIZING POWER OUR SACRED CAUSE AND CONVEY VISION ITS SPIRITUAL AND SOCIALLY CONSTRUCTIVE BENEFITS TO YOUR COMPATRIOTS OF ALL AGES.

17 March 1983

* * * * *

Now is an opportunity to awaken the interest, set afire the hearts and enlist the active support of young people of every nation, class and creed in that continent. The key to success in this endeavour is, firstly, to deepen your understanding of the Teachings of the Cause so that you will be able to apply them to the problems of individuals and society, and explain them to your peers in ways that they will understand and welcome; secondly, to strive to model your behaviour in every way after the high standards of honesty, trustworthiness, courage, loyalty, forbearance, purity and spirituality set forth in the Teachings; and above all, to live in continual awareness of the presence and all-conquering power of Bahá'u'lláh, which will enable you to overcome every temptation and surmount every obstacle.

4 July 1983

* * * * *

May you all persevere in your individual efforts to teach the Faith, but with added zest, to study the Writings, but with greater earnestness. May you pursue your education and training for future service to mankind, offering as much of your free time as possible to activities on behalf of the Cause. May those of you already bent on your life's work and who may have already founded families, strive toward becoming the living embodiments of Bahá'í ideals, both in the spiritual nurturing of your families and in your active involvement in the efforts on the home front or abroad in the pioneering field. May all respond to the current demands upon the Faith by displaying a fresh measure of dedication to the tasks at hand.

3 January 1984

* * * * *

The present requirements of a Faith whose responsibilities rapidly increase in relation to its rise from obscurity impose an inescapable duty on the youth to ensure that their lives reflect to a marked degree the transforming power of the new Revelation they have embraced. Otherwise, by what example are the claims of Bahá'u'lláh to be judged? How is His healing message to be acknowledged by a sceptical humanity if it produces no noticeable effect upon the young, who are seen to be among the most energetic, the most pliable and promising elements in any society?

8 May 1985

* * * * *

The words, the deeds, the attitudes, the lack of prejudice, the nobility of character, the high sense of service to others — in a word, those qualities and actions which distinguish a Bahá'í must unfailingly characterize their inner life and outer behaviour, and their interactions with friends or foe.

8 May 1985

*****

URGE CONFERENCE PARTICIPANTS CONSIDER MEANS BY WHICH YOU CAN SHOW TO PEERS EFFECT OF HIGH MORAL STANDARDS IN PROMOTING TRUE LIBERTY ABIDING HAPPINESS, AND CAN RESTORE TO MANKIND APPRECIATION SPIRITUAL BASIS PURPOSE HUMAN LIFE.

4 August 1987

* * * * *

Those of you who are at a point in your studies or careers where you can devote a special period of service to the Cause of God, may be able to respond to the call of the Youth Council for an army of youth-year-of-service volunteers to go out after these conferences to accelerate the winning of the goals of the Three Year Plan in Europe. Those who cannot serve in this way, have other avenues of service in their own countries and abroad. For all of you there is the opportunity and the need to present the Teachings of the Cause to all whom you meet, through your character, your behaviour, your unity, your deeds and your words, and to win their allegiance to the Faith.

17 May 1994

Further reading on this topic:

Bahá'u'lláh, cited by Shoghi Effendi, *The Advent of Divine Justice*, 1st pocket-sized ed. (Wilmette, Ill: Bahá'í Publishing Trust, 1990) pp. 67-68.

Bahá'u'lláh, *Gleanings from the Writings of Bahá'u'lláh*, comp. and trans. Shoghi Effendi, rev. ed. (London: Bahá'í Publishing Trust, 1978), section XCIX, p. 199.

Bahá'u'lláh, *Tablets of Bahá'u'lláh revealed after the Kitáb-i-Aqdas*, comp. Research Department of the Universal House of Justice, trans. Habib Taherzadeh with the assistance of a Committee at the Bahá'í World Centre, 1st US hardcover ed. (Wilmette, Ill: Bahá'í Publishing Trust, 1993), pp. 161-2.

`Abdu'l-Bahá, *Some Answered Questions*, comp. and trans. Laura Clifford Barney, 1st pocket size ed. (Wilmette, Ill: Bahá'í Publishing Trust, 1984), p. 8.

The Báb, cited by Nabíl-A'zám in *The Dawn-Breakers: Nabíl's Narrative of the Early Days of the Bahá'í Revelation*, translated from the original Persian by Shoghi Effendi (London: Bahá'í Publishing Trust, 1932), pp. 63-5.

[B]

Qualities of the Youth

In country after country the achievements of Bahá'í youth are increasingly advancing the work of the Nine Year plan and arousing the admiration of their fellow believers. From the very beginning of the Bahá'í Era, youth have played a vital part in the promulgation of God's Revelation. The Báb Himself was but twenty-five years old when He declared His Mission, while many of the Letters of the Living were even younger. The Master, as a very young man, was called upon to shoulder heavy responsibilities in the service of His Father in 'Iraq and Turkey; and His brother, the Purest Branch, yielded up his life to God in the Most Great Prison at the age of twenty-two that the servants of God might 'be quickened, and all that dwell on earth be united.' Shoghi Effendi was a student at Oxford when called to the throne of his Guardianship, and many of the Knights of Bahá'u'lláh, who won imperishable fame during the Ten Year Crusade, were young people. Let it, therefore, never be imagined that youth must await their years of maturity before they can render invaluable services to the Cause of God.

For any person, whether Bahá'í or not, his youthful years are those in which he will make many decisions which will set the course of his life. In these years he is most likely to choose his life's work, complete his education, begin to earn his own living, marry, and start to raise his own family. Most important of all, it is during this period that the mind is most questing and that the spiritual values that will guide the person's future behaviour are adopted. These factors present Bahá'í youth with their greatest opportunities, their greatest challenges, and their greatest tests — opportunities to truly apprehend the teachings of their Faith and to give them to their contemporaries, challenges to overcome the pressures of the world and to provide leadership for their and succeeding generations, and tests enabling them to exemplify in their lives the high moral standards set forth in the Bahá'í writings. Indeed, the Guardian wrote of the Bahá'í youth that it is they 'who can contribute so decisively to the virility, the purity, and the driving force of the life of the Bahá'í community and upon whom must depend the future orientation of its destiny, and the complete unfoldment of the potentialities with which God has endowed it.'

10 June 1966

* * * * *

In the two years since we last addressed the youth of the Bahá'í world many remarkable advances have been made in the fortunes of the Faith. Not the least of these is the enrolment under the banner of Bahá'u'lláh of a growing army of young men and women eager to serve His Cause. The zeal, the enthusiasm, the steadfastness and the devotion of the youth in every land has brought great joy and assurance to our hearts.

During the last days of August and the first days of September, when nearly two thousand believers from all over the world gathered in the Holy Land to commemorate the Centenary of Bahá'u'lláh's arrival on these sacred shores, we had an opportunity to observe at first hand those qualities of good character, selfless service and determined effort exemplified in the youth who served as volunteer helpers, and we wish to express our gratitude for their loving assistance and for their example.

9 October 1968

* * * * *

AT THIS HOUR OF AFFLICTION AND GRIEF, AND AS WE APPROACH ANNIVERSARY MARTYRDOM BLESSED BAB CALL ON BAHA'I YOUTH TO REDEDICATE THEMSELVES TO URGENT NEEDS CAUSE BAHA'U'LLAH. LET THEM RECALL BLESSINGS HE PROMISED THOSE WHO IN PRIME OF YOUTH WILL ARISE TO ADORN THEIR HEARTS WITH HIS LOVE AND REMAIN STEADFAST AND FIRM. LET THEM CALL TO MIND EXPECTATIONS MASTER FOR EACH TO BE A FEARLESS LION, A MUSK-LADEN BREEZE WAFTING OVER MEADS VIRTUES. LET THEM MEDITATE OVER UNIQUE QUALITIES YOUTH SO GRAPHICALLY MENTIONED IN WRITINGS GUARDIAN WHO PRAISED THEIR ENTERPRISING AND ADVENTUROUS SPIRIT, AND THEIR VIGOUR, THEIR ALERTNESS, OPTIMISM AND EAGERNESS, AND THEIR DIVINELY APPOINTED, HOLY AND ENTHRALLING TASKS. WE FERVENTLY PRAY AT SACRED THRESHOLD THAT ARMY OF SPIRITUALLY AWAKENED AND DETERMINED YOUTH MAY IMMEDIATELY ARISE RESPONSE NEEDS PRESENT HOUR DEVOTE IN EVER GREATER MEASURE THEIR VALUED ENERGIES TO PROMOTE BOTH ON HOMEFRONTS AND IN FOREIGN FIELDS, CAUSE THEIR ALL-WATCHFUL AND EXPECTANT LORD. MAY THEY MANIFEST SAME SPIRIT SO RECENTLY EVINCED THEIR MARTYR BRETHREN CRADLE FAITH, SCALE SUCH HEIGHTS OF

ENDEAVOURS AS TO BECOME PRIDE THEIR PEERS CONSOLATION HEARTS PERSIAN BELIEVERS, AND DEMONSTRATE THAT THE FLAME HIS OMNIPOTENT HAND HAS KINDLED BURNS EVER BRIGHTER AND THAT ITS LIFE-IMPARTING WARMTH AND RADIANCE SHALL SOON ENVELOP PERMEATE WHOLE EARTH.

24 June 1983

* * * * *

THE EXHORTATIONS ESPECIALLY ADDRESSED TO YOUTH BY OUR BELOVED MASTER AND THE GALVANIZING INFLUENCE OF THE GUARDIAN'S GUIDANCE WILL ECHO EVEN MORE LOUDLY IN YOUR HEARTS NOW. INDEED WE WILL PRAY ARDENTLY AT THE HOLY SHRINES THAT YOU MAY REALIZE IN YOUR LIVES THE IDEALS THEY SO PERSISTENTLY UPHELD, THAT YOU MAY THUS 'ACQUIRE BOTH INNER AND OUTER PERFECTIONS' AS YOU INCREASE YOUR STUDY OF THE HEAVENLY WRITINGS, STRIVE TOWARDS EXCELLENCE IN THE SCIENCES AND ARTS AND BECOME KNOWN FOR YOUR INDEPENDENCE OF SPIRIT, YOUR KNOWLEDGE AND YOUR SELF-CONTROL. MAY YOU, AS ABDU'L-BAHA WISHED, BE 'FIRST AMONG THE PURE, THE FREE AND THE WISE.'

24 August 1984

* * * * *

Rejecting the low sights of mediocrity, let them scale the ascending heights of excellence in all they aspire to do. May they resolve to elevate the very atmosphere in which they move, whether it be in the school rooms or halls of higher learning, in their work, their recreation, their Bahá'í activity or social service.

8 May 1985

* * * * *

84

LOVING GREETINGS TO PARTICIPANTS OF THIS CONFERENCE CONVENED AT TIME WHEN EUROPEAN BAHA'IS HAVE UNPRECEDENTED OPPORTUNITY DEMONSTRATE POWER FAITH ERADICATE BARRIERS INTERNATIONAL COOPERATION AND INFUSE DYNAMIC OPTIMISTIC QUALITIES INTO COMMUNITY WHICH HAS ALREADY MADE SUCH HISTORIC CONTRIBUTION ADVANCEMENT MANKIND.

EUROPEAN BAHA'I YOUTH DISTINGUISHED BY ENERGY VITALITY AND ENTHUSIASM CAN MAKE DISTINCTIVE CONTRIBUTION EMERGENCE FAITH AS PRIMARY AGENT PROMOTING WORLD ORDER AND CIVILISATION.

4 August 1987

* * * * *

To be young is not easy. There are so many calls on one's time and energy because, not only are you summoned to perform the duties of the day, but also to prepare yourselves for the tasks which will be yours during the remainder of your lives. In weighing how to apportion your time and energy to such a multitude of activities you can all upon the power of consultation with your parents, your friends, and the divinely created institutions of the Bahá'í administration.

17 May 1994

* * * * *

Further reading on this topic:
Bahá'u'lláh, cited by the Universal House of Justice, Ridván message to the Bahá'ís of the world, 1982.
'Abdu'l-Bahá, cited by Bahá'í National Youth Committee (comp.) in *Unrestrained as the Wind: A Life Dedicated to Bahá'u'lláh* (Wilmette, Ill: Bahá'í Publishing Trust, 1985), p. 21
Shoghi Effendi, *The Advent of Divine Justice*, pp. 18; 58.

[C]

Call to Service
(Teaching & Development)

The second field of service, which is linked intimately with the first, is teaching the Faith, particularly to their fellow youth, among whom are some of the most open and seeking minds in the world. Not yet having acquired all the responsibilities of a family or a long-established home and job, youth can the more easily choose where they will live and study or work. In the world at large young people travel hither and thither seeking amusement, education, and experiences. Bahá'í youth, bearing the incomparable treasure of the Word of God for this Day, can harness this mobility into service for mankind and can choose their places of residence, their areas of travel, and their types of work with the goal in mind of how they can best serve the Faith.

10 June 1966

* * * * *

Paralleling the growth of his inner life through prayer, meditation, service, and study of the teachings, Bahá'í youth have the opportunity to learn in practice the very functioning of the Order of Bahá'u'lláh. Through taking part in conferences and summer schools as well as Nineteen Day Feasts, and in service on committees, they can develop the wonderful skill of Bahá'í consultation, thus tracing new paths of human corporate action. Consultation is no easy skill to learn, requiring as it does the subjugation of all egotism and unruly passions, the cultivation of frankness and freedom of thought as well as courtesy, openness of mind, and wholehearted acquiescence in a majority decision. In this field Bahá'í youth may demonstrate the efficiency, the vigour, the access of unity which arise from true consultation and, by contrast, demonstrate the futility of partisanship, lobbying, debate, secret diplomacy, and unilateral action which characterize modern affairs. Youth also take part in the life of the Bahá'í community as a whole and promote a society in which all generations — elderly, middle-aged, youth, children — are fully integrated and make up an organic whole. By refusing to carry over the antagonisms and mistrust between the generations which perplex and bedevil modern Society, they will again demonstrate the healing and life-giving nature of their religion.

10 June 1966

* * * * *

You who are now gathered in Namur in response to the call sent out by the Continental Board of Counsellors have been made responsible for working out the next stages of this audacious campaign, within the framework already agreed between Counsellors and the National Spiritual Assemblies, and you may be sure that our prayers will surround you as we supplicate the Blessed Beauty to inspire your deliberations, unite your hearts and fire your enthusiasm so that there may go out from this conference a ringing call, carefully conceived plans and clearly stated objectives, that will not only galvanize the youth of the continent but, through them, impart a mighty surge forward to the teaching work of the entire European Bahá'í Community.

It is our earnest hope that the outriders of this youthful army of Bahá'u'lláh will win such victories by the time of the Conference in Fiesch as will so inspire the far larger band of young Bahá'ís who will be gathered there that a wave of achievement, which will have already started to roll, will at that conference gain speed and magnitude and revolutionize the progress of the Cause in Europe.

Let those who set their hand to this vital enterprise press confidently forward, undeterred by any obstacles which may stand in their way, joyously assured of the unfailing assistance of the conquering power of Bahá'u'lláh, Whom we will supplicate to guide and reinforce every step you take for the promotion of His Cause.

29 March 1971

* * * * *

Our hopes for your two-year campaign are boundless, and visualise nothing less than a tremendous forward surge in the spiritual revival referred to by our beloved Guardian. Our confidence in your ability to perform the task is unshakeable, and we assure you of our firm conviction that your efforts will be assisted by God to the degree to which your supplications and sacrifices are poured forth in His path.

Dear friends, we delight in your enthusiasm, admire your accomplishments, give thanks for your dedication and pray that an ever-increasing outpouring of divine bounties and confirmations may reward your efforts in the service of the Blessed Beauty.

16 July 1971

* * * * *

A vibrant band of Bahá'í youth on the European continent, committed to the promotion of the Cause of Bahá'u'lláh and the upholding of His laws and principles, determined to work in harmony and unity with their fellow believers of all ages and classes, can revolutionize the progress of the Cause. With a rapid increase in the size of the Bahá'í communities in Europe, the believers of that continent, the cradle of western civilisation, will be the better able to serve as a fountainhead of pioneers, travelling teachers and financial assistants to the Bahá'í communities of the Third World.

4 July 1983

* * * * *

A particular challenge to the Bahá'í Youth of Europe is the vast Eastern half of the continent that is as yet scarcely touched by the light of the Faith of Bahá'u'lláh. It is not easy to settle in those lands, but with ingenuity, determination and reliance upon the confirmations of Bahá'u'lláh, it is certainly possible both to settle and to persevere in service, in goals which demand a spirit of self-sacrifice, detachment and purity of heart worthy of those who would emulate the shining example set by the Martyrs in Iran, so many of whom are youth who have given their lives rather than breathe one word that would be a betrayal of the Trust of God placed upon them.

With love and utmost longing we call upon you to immerse yourselves in the Divine Teachings, champion the Cause of God and His Law, and arise for the quickening of mankind.

4 July 1983

* * * * *

EUROPEAN BAHA'I COMMUNITY HAS DISTINGUISHED RECORD FORMATIVE AGE DEMONSTRATING STRENGTH AND ACTIVITY ITS ADMINISTRATIVE INSTITUTIONS WITH FIDELITY AND PERSEVERANCE ITS ADHERENTS. BY FULL PARTICIPATION IN BAHA'I COMMUNITY LIFE YOUTH CAN FURTHER ENHANCE THIS ENVIABLE RECORD. FROM SEEDS SOWN DURING MANY DECADES DEVOTED EFFORTS TEACHING FAITH, YOUTH CAN NOW GATHER BOUNTIFUL HARVEST.

4 August 1987

* * * * *

The time has now come for the European believers, most especially the Bahá'í youth, to take full advantage of the growing receptivity to the Bahá'í teachings now evident in Europe. The people of this continent are yearning for the tranquillity, harmony and peace which can be established on an enduring foundation only through the erection of the World Order of Bahá'u'lláh. Through well-conceived, energetically-pursued and sustained teaching campaigns the youth can hasten the advent of that day when their continent will be blessed with entry by troops and the foundation laid for the spiritual revolution in Europe, anticipated by Shoghi Effendi.

We look forward with eager anticipation to European Bahá'í youth arising with a renewed surge of energy and dedication to commit themselves fully in pursuit of the goals of the Six Year Plan. Exciting and challenging vistas are open before them, not only on the homefront of western Europe, but also in eastern Europe where the social changes now occurring must lead eventually to freedom to teach the Faith and establish its institutions. There are vital needs in Africa which the youth in Europe can assist in meeting, renewing and strengthening the historical links binding these two great continents.

12 July 1988

* * * * *

Further reading on this topic:

Bahá'u'lláh, cited by Shoghi Effendi in *The Advent of Divine Justice*, pp. 69-71; 84.

Bahá'u'lláh, *Gleanings*, sections LXXI (pp. 136-8); CXXVIII (pp. 274-8).

`Abdu'l-Bahá, *Tablets of the Divine Plan*, 1st pocket size ed. (Wilmette, Ill: Bahá'í Publishing Trust, 1993), pp. 47-55.

[D]

A Special Service

Many of them offered to pioneer, but one perplexing question recurred: Shall I continue my education, or should I pioneer now? Undoubtedly this same question is in the mind of every young Bahá'í wishing to dedicate his life to the advancement of the Faith. There is no stock answer which applies to all situations; the beloved Guardian gave different answers to different individuals on this question. Obviously circumstances vary with each individual case. Each individual must decide how he can best serve the Cause. In making this decision, it will be helpful to weigh the following factors:

Upon becoming a Bahá'í one's whole life is, or should become devoted to the progress of the Cause of God, and every talent or faculty he possesses is ultimately committed to this overriding life objective. Within this framework he must consider, among other things, whether by continuing his education now he can be a more effective pioneer later, or alternatively whether the urgent need for pioneers, while possibilities for teaching are still open, outweighs an anticipated increase in effectiveness. This is not an easy decision, since oftentimes the spirit which prompts the pioneering offer is more important than one's academic attainments. One's liability for military service may be a factor in timing the offer of pioneer service.

One may have outstanding obligations to others, including those who may be dependent on him for support. It may be possible to combine a pioneer project with a continuing educational program. Consideration may also be given to the possibility that a pioneering experience, even though it interrupts the formal educational program, may prove beneficial in the long run in that studies would later be resumed with a more mature outlook. The urgency of a particular goal which one is especially qualified to fill and for which there are no other offers. The fact that the need for pioneers will undoubtedly be with us for many generations to come, and that therefore there will be many calls in future for pioneering service.

The principle of consultation also applies. One may have the obligation to consult others, such as one's parents, one's Local and National Assemblies, and the pioneering committees.

Finally, bearing in mind the principle of sacrificial service and the unfailing promises Bahá'u'lláh ordained for those who arise to serve His Cause, one should pray and meditate on what his course of action will be. Indeed, it often happens that the answer will be found in no other way.

9 October 1968

* * * * *

In the light of experience, however, it is now clear that we should have no misgivings in encouraging young Bahá'ís to enrol in such voluntary service organization programmes as the United Nations Volunteers, United States Peace Corps, Canadian University Services Overseas (CUSO) and similar Canadian agencies, the British Volunteer Programme (BVP) of the United Kingdom, and other voluntary service organizations. Other countries such as Germany, the Netherlands, and the Scandinavian lands are understood to have similar service organizations which are compatible with Bahá'í development goals as now tentatively envisaged.

Some of the advantages of such service to the Faith are worth mentioning. Volunteers will receive thorough orientation and sometimes will be taught basic skills which will enable them to help the Bahá'í community in projects undertaken in developing countries. Wherever they serve, these volunteers should be able to participate in Bahá'í activities, and contribute to the consolidation of the Bahá'í community. The freedom to teach is to a large extent dependent upon the local interpretation of the group leader, but even if volunteers do not engage in direct teaching, being known as Bahá'ís and showing the Bahá'í spirit and attitude towards work and service should attract favourable attention and may, in many instances, be instrumental in attracting individuals to the Faith of Bahá'u'lláh. And finally, the period of overseas service often produces a taste for such service, and volunteers may well offer to directly promote the pioneer work either in the same country or in another developing country.

13 December 1983

* * * * *

Further to these aspirations is the need for a mighty mobilization of teaching activities reflecting regularity in the patterns of service rendered by young Bahá'ís. The native urge of youth to move from place to place, combined with their abounding zeal, indicates that you can become more deliberately and numerously involved in these activities as travelling teachers. One pattern of this mobilization could be short-term projects, carried out at home or in other lands, dedicated to both teaching the Faith and improving the living conditions of people. Another could be that, while still young and unburdened by family responsibilities, you give attention to the idea of volunteering a set period, say one or two years, to some Bahá'í service, on the home front or abroad, in the teaching or development field. It would accrue to the strength and stability of the community if such patterns could be followed by succeeding generations of youth. Regardless of the modes of service, however, youth must be understood to be fully engaged, at all times, in all climes and under all conditions. In your varied pursuits you may rest assured of the loving support and guidance of the Bahá'í institutions operating at every level.

3 January 1984

* * * * *

There is one comment that the Universal House of Justice has asked us to make in relation to a number of points made in the analysis, since this may assist in overcoming the problem of the bewildering range of alternatives that lie before youth in these days. This is the importance of conveying to the youth the awareness that every aspect of a person's life is an element of his or her service to Bahá'u'lláh: the love and respect one has for one's parents; the pursuit of one's education; the nurturing of good health; the acquiring of a trade of profession; one's behaviour towards others and the upholding of a high moral standard; one's marriage and the bringing up of one's children; one's activities in teaching the Faith and the building up the strength of the Bahá'í community whether this be in such simple matters as attending the Nineteen Day Feast or the observance of the Bahá'í Holy Days, or in more demanding tasks required by service in the administration of the Faith; and, not least, to take time each day to read the Writings and say the Obligatory Prayer, which are the source of growing spiritual strength, understanding, and attachment to God. The concept of the Youth Year of Service should be viewed in this context, as a special service that the youth can devote to the Cause, and which should prove to be a highly valuable element in their own spiritual and intellectual development. It is not an alternative to, or in conflict with, the carrying out of the other vital tasks enumerated above, but rather a unique service and privilege which should be combined with them in the way that is best suited to each individual case.

7 December 1992

* * * * *

Those of you who are at a point in your studies or careers where you can devote a special period of service to the Cause of God, may be able to respond to the call of the Youth Council for an army of youth-year-of-service volunteers to go out after these conferences to accelerate the winning of the goals of the Three Year Plan in Europe. Those who cannot serve in this way, have other avenues of service in their own countries and abroad. For all of you there is the opportunity and the need to present the Teachings of the Cause to all whom you meet, through your character, your behaviour, your unity, your deeds and your words, and to win their allegiance to the Faith.

17 May 1994

* * * * *

[E]

Sacrifice

RECENT MARTYRDOMS COURAGEOUS STEADFAST YOUTH IN SHIRAZ, SCENE INAUGURATION MISSION MARTYR-PROPHET, REMINISCENT ACTS VALOUR YOUTHFUL IMMORTALS HEROIC AGE. CONFIDENT BAHÁ'Í YOUTH THIS GENERATION WILL NOT ALLOW THIS FRESH BLOOD SHED ON VERY SOIL WHERE FIRST WAVE PERSECUTION FAITH TOOK PLACE REMAIN UNVINDICATED OR THIS SUBLIME SACRIFICE UNAVAILING.

24 June 1983

* * * * *

For the sake of preserving such virtues much innocent blood has been shed in the past, and much, even today, is being sacrificed in Iran by young and old alike. Consider, for example, the instances in S̲h̲íráz last summer of the six young women, their ages ranging from 18 to 25 years, whose lives were snuffed out by the hangman's noose. All faced attempted inducements to recant their Faith; all refused to deny their Beloved. Look also at the accounts of the astounding fortitude shown over and over again by children and youth who were subjected to the interrogations and abuses of teachers and mullahs and were expelled from school for upholding their beliefs. It, moreover, bears noting that under the restrictions so cruelly imposed on their community, the youth rendered signal services, placing their energies at the disposal of Bahá'í institutions throughout the country. No splendour of speech could give more fitting testimony to their spiritual commitment and fidelity than these pure acts of selflessness and devotion. In virtually no other place on earth is so great a price for faith required of Bahá'ís. Nor could there be found more willing, more radiant bearers of the cup of sacrifice than the valiant Bahá'í youth of Iran. Might it, then, not be reasonably expected that you, the youth and young adults living at such an extraordinary time, witnessing such stirring examples of the valour of your Iranian fellows, and exercising such freedom of movement, would sally forth, 'unrestrained as the wind,' in the field of Bahá'í action?

3 January 1984

* * * * *

OUR HEARTS LEAP AT THE INNUMERABLE IMMEDIATE OPPORTUNITIES FOR THE FURTHER UNFOLDMENT OF THE ORDER OF BAHA'U'LLAH TO WHICH UNDOUBTEDLY, YOU CAN AND WILL APPLY YOUR ABUNDANT TALENTS, YOUR ZEST FOR ACTION AND, ABOVE ALL, THE ENTHUSIASM OF YOUR DEVOTION. SURELY, YOU WILL SEE

THAT THE HEROIC DEEDS OF SACRIFICE ON THE PART OF YOUR
IRANIAN BRETHREN ARE MATCHED WITH CORRESPONDING EFFORTS
ON YOUR PART IN THE VAST FIELDS OF TEACHING AND SERVICE
LYING OPEN BEFORE YOU.

24 August 1984

* * * * *

Further reading on this topic:

Bahá'u'lláh, cited in *Unrestrained as the Wind*, p. 18.
`Abdu'l-Bahá, cited ibid., pp. 18-19.
Shoghi Effendi, cited ibid., pp. 19-20.

[F]

Attracting our Peers

SITUATION THUS PRESENTS BAHA'I YOUTH WITH GREAT
OPPORTUNITIES INESCAPABLE CHALLENGE TO RESCUE THEIR PEERS
FROM SLOUGH DESPONDENCY POINTING THEM TOWARDS
HOPE-RESTORING BANNER MOST GREAT NAME. HOW FITTING THEN
THAT YOU SHOULD CONSIDER AT THESE CONFERENCES BEST MEANS
EQUIP YOURSELVES SPIRITUALLY TO FULFIL TEACHING MISSION
PARTICULARLY SUITED TO YOUR CAPACITIES FOR SERVICE, YOUR
ABOUNDING ZEAL AND ENERGY.

17 March 1983

* * * * *

A highlight of this period of the Seven Year Plan has been the
phenomenal proclamation accorded the Faith in the wake of the
unabating persecutions in Iran; a new interest in its Teachings has
been aroused on a wide scale. Simultaneously, more and more
people from all strata of society frantically seek their true

identity, which is to say, although they would not so plainly admit it, the spiritual meaning of their lives; prominent among these seekers are the young. Not only does this knowledge open fruitful avenues for Bahá'í initiative, it also indicates to young Bahá'ís a particular responsibility so to teach the Cause and live the life as to give vivid expression to those virtues that would fulfill the spiritual yearning of their peers.

3 January 1984

* * * * *

The dark horizon faced by a world which has failed to recognize the Promised One, the Source of its salvation, acutely affects the outlook of the younger generations; their distressing lack of hope and their indulgence in desperate but futile and even dangerous solutions make a direct claim on the remedial attention of Bahá'í youth, who, through their knowledge of that Source and the bright vision with which they have thus been endowed, cannot hesitate to impart to their despairing fellow youth the restorative joy, the constructive hope, the radiant assurances of Bahá'u'lláh's stupendous Revelation.

8 May 1985

* * * * *

You have come together from lands which are troubled by many different ills: ecological, economic, political, social, intellectual and, above all, moral and spiritual. You are aware that some of your peers are desperately seeking solutions and, too often alas, are driven to violent means to combat those immediate evils which fill their vision. Others turn aside, despairingly or cynically from any thought that a remedy is possible. You know the solution, you have the vision, you have he guidance and you are the recipients of the spiritual power which can enable you to triumph over all adversities and bring new life to the youth of Europe.

17 May 1994

* * * * *

Further reading on this topic:
Shoghi Effendi, *The Advent of Divine Justice*, p. 58.
Shoghi Effendi, cited in *Unrestrained as the Wind*, p. 99.

[G]

Correlation of the Bahá'í Teachings with Modern Thought

When studying at school or university Bahá'í youth will often find themselves in the unusual and slightly embarrassing position of having a more profound insight into a subject than their instructors. The Teachings of Bahá'u'lláh throw light on so many aspects of human life and knowledge that a Bahá'í must learn, earlier than most, to weigh the information that is given to him rather than to accept it blindly. A Bahá'í has the advantage of the Divine Revelation for this age, which shines like a searchlight on so many problems that baffle modern thinkers; he must therefore develop the ability to learn everything from those around him, showing proper humility before his teachers, but always relating what he hears to the Bahá'í teachings, for they will enable him to sort out the gold from the dross of human error.

10 June 1966

* * * * *

BURGEONING TEACHING OPPORTUNITIES EUROPE NECESSITATE GREATER EFFORT BELIEVERS CORRELATE TEACHINGS WITH CURRENT THOUGHT AND NEEDS ALL PEOPLE, THUS SHOWING BAHA'I REVELATION SOLE REMEDY INNUMERABLE ILLS AFFLICTING PRESENT SOCIETY.

4 August 1987

* * * * *

Further reading on this topic:

Bahá'u'lláh, Gleanings, sections XVI (pp. 38-40); XXXIV (pp. 77-81); CXX (pp. 253-4).

Shoghi Effendi, 'The Goal of a New World Order', in *The World Order of Bahá'u'lláh: Selected Letters,* 1st pocket-sized ed. (Wilmette, Ill: Bahá'í Publishing Trust, 1991), pp. 29-48.

Shoghi Effendi, cited in Shaping Your Future, p. 25

Letter written on behalf of Shoghi Effendi, cited in Rúhíyyih Rabbani, *The Priceless Pearl* (London: Bahá'í Publishing Trust, 1969), pp. 212-13.

The Universal House of Justice, 'The Challenge and Promise of Bahá'í Scholarship', in *The Bahá'í World: An International Record*, prepared under the supervision of the Universal House of Justice, vol. XVII (133, 134 and 135 of the Bahá'í Era, 1976-1979), (Haifa: Bahá'í World Centre, 1981), pp. 195-6.

[H]

Condition of the World
(Integration & Disintegration)

Those who now are in their teens and twenties are faced with a special challenge and can seize an opportunity that is unique in human history. During the Ten Year Crusade — the ninth part of that majestic process described so vividly by our beloved Guardian — the community of the Most Great Name spread with the speed of lightning over the major territories and islands of the globe, increased manifoldly its manpower and resources, saw the beginning of the entry of the peoples by troops into the Cause of God, and completed the structure of the Administrative Order of Bahá'u'lláh. Now, firmly established in the world, the Cause, in the opening years of the tenth part of that same process, is perceptibly emerging from the obscurity that has, for the most part, shrouded it since its inception and is arising to challenge the outworn concepts of a corrupt society and proclaim the solution for the agonizing problems of a disordered humanity. During the lifetime of those who are now young the condition of the world, and the place of the Bahá'í Cause in it, will change immeasurably, for we are entering a highly critical phase in this era of transition.

10 June 1966

* * * * *

The course of history has brought to your generation an unprecedented opportunity and challenge. The rejection of the old world by the youth, in all countries, is shared by Bahá'ís and non-Bahá'ís alike. Unlike your non-Bahá'í contemporaries, however, you have something to put in its place — the World Order of Bahá'u'lláh.

That Bahá'í youth are fully capable of meeting the challenge which evolution has placed before them has already been demonstrated. Now, in this conference at Fiesch, as you gird yourselves to launch a campaign in Europe — a continent which has 'entered upon what may well be regarded as the opening phase of a great spiritual revival that bids fair to eclipse any period in its spiritual history' — we urge you to consider that the more you understand the purpose of Bahá'u'lláh and the method by which He will achieve this purpose the greater will be your success.

16 July 1971

* * * * *

YOU MEET AT HIGHLY CRITICAL MOMENT HISTORY WHEN TURMOIL ASSOCIATED WITH THIS ERA OF TRANSITION INTENSIFIES. WITHIN CAUSE ITSELF CAN BE SEEN ON ONE HAND UNPRECEDENTED CAMPAIGN PERSECUTION LONG-SUFFERING IRANIAN BRETHREN AND ON OTHER HAND RESOUNDING TRIUMPHS SEVEN YEAR PLAN INDUCED BY THEIR SACRIFICES AND SYMBOLIZED BY OCCUPANCY PERMANENT SEAT UNIVERSAL HOUSE OF JUSTICE. MANKIND RAPIDLY APPROACHES RECKONING WITH BAHA'U'LLAH'S INJUNCTION THAT IT BE UNITED. FROM FAR AND NEAR ANGUISHED MULTITUDES CRY FOR PEACE BUT BEING LARGELY IGNORANT HIS LIFE-REDEEMING MESSAGE THEY FEEL NO HOPE.

17 March 1983

* * * * *

ESSENTIAL THAT YOUTH PROLONGED SYSTEMATIC STUDY WRITINGS BELOVED GUARDIAN ACQUIRE PROFOUND UNDERSTANDING OPERATION OF FORCES OF DECLINE AND GROWTH CREATING UNIVERSAL FERMENT IN WORLD TODAY AND LEADING MANKIND FORWARD TO GLORIOUS DESTINY.

4 August 1987

* * * * *

You have come together from lands which are troubled by many different ills: ecological, economic, political, social, intellectual and, above all, moral and spiritual. You are aware that some of your peers are desperately seeking solutions and, too often alas, are driven to violent means to combat those immediate evils which fill their vision. Others turn aside, despairingly or cynically from any thought that a remedy is possible. You know the solution, you have the vision, you have he guidance and you are the recipients of the spiritual power which can enable you to triumph over all adversities and bring new life to the youth of Europe.

17 May 1994

* * * * *

Further reading on this topic:

Bahá'u'lláh, *Gleanings*, sections IV (pp. 6-7); LXX (pp. 135-6). Shoghi Effendi, 'The Goal of a New World Order', *World Order*, pp. 29-48.

[I]

Shaping Society

This generation of Bahá'í youth enjoys a unique distinction. You will live your lives in a period when the forces of history are moving to a climax, when mankind will see the establishment of the Lesser Peace, and during which the Cause of God will play an increasingly prominent role in the reconstruction of human society. It is you who will be called upon in the years to come to stand at the helm of the Cause in face of conditions and developments which can, as yet, scarcely be imagined.

4 July 1983

* * * * *

These expectations reinforce the immediate, vast opportunities begging our attention. To visualize, however imperfectly, the challenges that engage us now, we have only to reflect, in the light of our sacred Writings, upon the confluence of favourable circumstances brought about by the accelerated unfolding of the Divine Plan over nearly five decades, by the untold potencies of the spiritual drama being played out in Iran, and by the creative energy stimulated by awareness of the approaching end of the twentieth century. Undoubtedly, it is within your power to contribute significantly to shaping the societies of the coming century; youth can move the world.

3 January 1984

* * * * *

We applaud those youth who, in respect of this period, have already engaged in some activity within their national and local communities or in collaboration with their peers in other countries, and call upon them to persevere in their unyielding efforts to acquire spiritual qualities and useful qualifications. For it they do so, the influence of their high-minded motivations will exert itself upon world developments conducive to a productive, progressive and peaceful future.

8 May 1985

* * * * *

EUROPEAN BAHA'I YOUTH DISTINGUISHED BY ENERGY VITALITY AND ENTHUSIASM CAN MAKE DISTINCTIVE CONTRIBUTION EMERGENCE FAITH AS PRIMARY AGENT PROMOTING WORLD ORDER AND CIVILISATION.

4 August 1987

* * * * *

Further reading on this topic:

`Abdu'l-Bahá, *Selections from the Writings of `Abdu'l-Bahá*, comp. Research Department of the Universal House of Justice, trans. a committee at the Bahá'í World Centre and by Marzieh Gail, rev. ed. (Haifa: Bahá'í World Centre, 1982), section 15, pp. 29-32.

Shoghi Effendi, 'The Unfoldment of World Civilization', *World Order*, pp. 161-206

[J]

Fields of Study

When studying at school or university Bahá'í youth will often find themselves in the unusual and slightly embarrassing position of having a more profound insight into a subject than their instructors. The Teachings of Bahá'u'lláh throw light on so many aspects of human life and knowledge that a Bahá'í must learn, earlier than most, to weigh the information that is given to him rather than to accept it blindly. A Bahá'í has the advantage of the Divine Revelation for this age, which shines like a searchlight on so many problems that baffle modern thinkers; he must therefore develop the ability to learn everything from those around him, showing proper humility before his teachers, but always relating what he hears to the Bahá'í teachings, for they will enable him to sort out the gold from the dross of human error.

10 June 1966

* * * * *

When deciding what course of training to follow, youth can consider acquiring those skills and professions that will be of benefit in education, rural development, agriculture, economics, technology, health, radio and in many other areas of endeavour that are so urgently needed in the developing countries of the World. You can also devote time in the midst of your studies, or other activities to, travel-teaching or service projects in the Third World.

4 July 1983

* * * * *

Indeed, let them welcome with confidence the challenges awaiting them. Imbued with this excellence and a corresponding humility, with tenacity and a loving servitude, today's youth must move towards the front ranks of the professions, trades, arts and crafts which are necessary to the further progress of humankind — this to ensure that the spirit of the Cause will cast its illumination on all these important areas of human endeavour. Moreover, while aiming at mastering the unifying concepts and swiftly advancing technologies of this era of communications, they can, indeed they must also guarantee the transmittal to the future of those skills which will preserve the marvellous, indispensable achievements of the past. The transformation which is to occur in the functioning of society will certainly depend to a great extent on the effectiveness of the preparations the youth make for the world they will inherit.

8 May 1985

Further reading on this topic:

Bahá'u'lláh, *Tablets*, pp. 51-2; 168-9.

`Abdu'l-Bahá, *The Secret of Divine Civilization*, trans. Marzieh Gail, 1st pocket size ed. (Wilmette, Ill: Bahá'í Publishing Trust, 1994), pp. 2-3.

`Abdu'l-Bahá, *Selections*, section 126, pp. 144-5.

`Abdu'l-Bahá, *Paris Talks: Addresses Given by `Abdu'l-Bahá in 1911*, 12th rev. ed. (London: Bahá'í Publishing Trust, 1995), pp. 32-4.

Shoghi Effendi, cited by Shahriar Razavi (comp.), in *Shaping Your Future: A compilation of extracts from the Bahá'í Writings on Work, Study and Service* (London: National Youth Committee of the National Spiritual Assembly of the Bahá'ís of the United Kingdom, 1989), pp. 25-6.

[K]

Preparation for Adult Life

The third field of service is the preparation by youth for their later years. It is the obligation of a Bahá'í to educate his children; likewise it is the duty of the children to acquire knowledge of the arts and sciences and to learn a trade or a profession whereby they, in turn, can earn their living and support their families. This, for a Bahá'í youth, is in itself a service to God, a service, moreover, which can be combined with teaching the Faith and often with pioneering. The Bahá'í community will need men and women of many skills and qualifications; for, as it grows in size the sphere of its activities in the life of society will increase and diversify. Let Bahá'í youth, therefore, consider the best ways in which they can use and develop their native abilities for the service of mankind and the Cause of God, whether this be as farmers, teachers, doctors, artisans, musicians, or any one of the multitude of livelihoods that are open to them.

10 June 1966

* * * * *

Further reading on this topic:

Bahá'u'lláh, `Abdu'l-Bahá, Shoghi Effendi and the Universal House of Justice, cited in *Shaping Your Future*, pp. 1-16.

Index

Messages from the Universal House of Justice are referenced by message number, followed by paragraph number.

Continental Board of Counsellors,
3.2, 14.2
courage, 7.2
courtesy, 1.9
crafts, 11.8
cynicism, 15.4

decadence, 1.5
decency, 1.5
dedication, 4.4
deeds, 15.6
deepening, 1.10
despair, 15.4
detachment, 1.5
determination, 7.5, 16.3
developing countries (Third
World), 7.3, 7.4, 8.4
development, 7.4, 8.3, 9.1, 9.8
devotion, 2.1
doubt, 16.6

East, 1.5
economics, 7.4
education, 1.2, 1.6, 1.8, 2.3-5, 7.4,
9.7, 14.3, 15.6
eagerness, 6
egotism, 1.9
energy, 5.2, 12.2
enrolment of youth, 2.1
enterprise, 6
enthusiasm, 2.1, 3.2, 4.4, 11.4,
12.2, 16.2
entry by troops, 1.3, 13.3
Europe, Bahá'ís, 3.2, 4.2, 7.3, 12.1,
12.5, 12.6, 13.2-3
youth, 3.1, 3.3, 4.4, 7.1-6,
12.2, 15.1,

blessings, 7.2
eastern, 7.5, 13.4, 16.1n
European Bahá'í Youth Council,
15.1, 15.6
evolution, 4.2
example, 5.3, 16.4
excellence, 10.3, 11.7-8

faculties, 2.4
family, 1.7, 9.7
fear, 16.6
forbearance, 7.2
frankness, 1.9
freedom, 10.3
of movement, 9.6
of thought, 1.9

God, 1.1, 1.2, 1.5, 1.6, 2.8, 16.6

happiness, 12.3
harmony, 13.3
health, 7.4, 14.3
history, 1.3, 4.1, 5.2, 7.1, 13.2
Holy Days, 14.3
honesty, 7.2
hope, 11.5, 16.4
humanity, 1.3, 5.2, 7.6, 11.8, 12.1,
15.2, 16.3, 16.6
humility, 1.8, 11.8

idealism, 16.2
independence of spirit, 10.3
ingenuity, 7.5
inner life, 1.9, 10.3, 11.6
International Year of Peace, 11.3
International Youth Year, 9.1-4,
11.1

126

Sh<u>í</u>ráz, 6, 9.6, 15.2

Shoghi Effendi, 1.1, 1.3, 2.3, 4.3,
    6, 10.3, 13.3
    quotations, 1.2, 4.2, 13.2
    writings, 12.4
skills, 1.7, 1.10
society, 1.3, 1.4, 1.5, 1.9, 7.1, 7.2,
    11.4, 11.8, 12.5, 15.4
Spiritual Assemblies,
    local, 2.6
    National, 2.6, 3.2, 8.2, 8.6, 14.2
spirituality, 1.5, 7.2, 11.2, 12.3,
    14.4
steadfastness, 6
summer schools, 1.9
supplications, 4.3

talents, 2.4, 10.2
teachers, 1.8
teaching the Faith, 1.6-7, 1.10, 2.4,
    3.2, 5.3, 6, 8.2, 8.4, 9.7, 9.8,
    10.2, 13.3, 13.5, 14.3, 16.3
    to peers, 1.2, 1.6, 1.10, 5.2, 7.2,
    15.4
tenacity, 11.8
tests, 1.2
trades, 1.7, 1.10, 11.8, 14.3

training, 7.4, 9.7
tranquillity, 13.3
transformation, 11.4, 11.8
travel, 1.6
travel teaching, 7.3, 7.4, 16.1n
twentieth century, 9.2
twenty-first century, 9.2, 16.2

United Nations, 9.1, 9.3
unity, 1.1, 1.2, 1.9, 3.2, 5.2, 7.3,
    8.4, 12.6, 14.3, 15.6
Universal House of Justice, 5.2
university, 1.8, 11.7

vigour, 6
virtues, 1.9
vision, 5.3, 11.5, 14.1, 15.4
vitality, 12.2
voluntary organizations, 8

West (Christendom), 1.5, 7.3
wisdom, 10.3
work, 1.6, 8.4, 11.7
world, 1.2, 1.3, 5.1, 12.2

zeal, 2.1, 5.2, 9.8, 16.2